Jackson's Chameleon, *Chamaeleo jacksonii xantholophus, male.*

Contents

Dedicated to Wendy and to the keikis of Hawai'i.

ACKNOWLEDGMENTS

A special mahalo to the following individuals who have shared information or otherwise contributed to this book: Wesley Chun, Jim Juvik, Spencer Tinker, Paul Breese, George Balazs, Duane Meier, Julie Nishioka Takaesu, Matt Walsh, Leighton Taylor, Allan Ziegler, Donald Hunsaker II, Norman Bezona, Pam Haley, Dwain Uyeda, Karla Kishinami, Charles Christensen, John Berger, Andrew J. Berger, Jack Throp, Bruce Carlson, Charles DeLuca, Ralph Alexander, James K. Baker, George V. Pickwell, Walter E. Meshaka, Jr., Kevin Izumi, James D. Lazell, Jr., Susan G. Brown, Mary Morgan, Ed Shallenberger, Masao Hanaoka, Mike Wong, Dick and Patti Bartlett, George R. Zug, Bill Love, Danté Fenolio, Michael Ready, Al Lam, Mike McCoy, Mike McCoid, Tihoti Maha'a, Tim and Amber Wright, James K. Baker, Peter C. H. Pritchard, Carl H. Ernst, Tommy Higashino, Steve Kaiser, Hiroshi Tagami, Robert Fisher, Bob Davignon, Louis Porras, Bob Hansen, David Crews, José P. Rosado, Douglas R. Mader, Greg Pregill, Philippe de Vosjoli, Gary Ferguson, Lee Grizmer, Anthony Wisnieski, Cecil Schwalbe, Richard C. Vogt, Darryl Amaral, Emilio M. Bruna, Jim Buskirk, Audrey Lupo, Glen Sahara, Steve Lane, Tim Lane, Mike Benedetti, David Perlowin, Andy Mansker, Jane Bowden-Manente and the late E. H. Bryan.

The author expresses his gratitude to the photographers who have contributed to this book, in particular, Grant K. Uchida, Dick Bartlett, Bill Love, George Balazs, Glyn Rogers, Peter C. H. Pritchard, Pat Briggs, Dennis Sheridan, Harold Cogger, Danny Rodriguez, Emilio M. Bruna, Sue Schafer-Severson, Ken Nemuras, Mark Hanlon, Tim Ohashi, Rick Hudson, Karl Frogner, and J. Sneed.

Introduction

The composition of Hawai'i's herpetofauna (reptiles and amphibians), while interwoven with the location, topography and flora of the islands, is primarily a result of human activity. Located near the middle of the Pacific Ocean, the Hawaiian Islands are isolated from the continents of North America and Asia by distances greater than 2,400 mi. (3,862 km). The climate is mild. Temperatures near sea level during the day average in the 80s to low 90s°F (27–34°C) during the six or seven "summer" months and in the 70s to low 80s°F (21–29°C) during the "winter" months. At areas of low elevation, there is typically a 10–15°F (5–8°C) drop at night. Temperatures at higher elevations are typically mild, with cool nighttime and winter temperatures only at areas of high elevation. Topography ranges from beach to tropical valley to high mountain slope. Rainfall over adjacent areas often differs markedly.

The Hawaiian Islands are volcanic in origin and have never been connected to any major landmass. The archipelago, consisting of more than 20 islands, extends in a fairly linear chain across 1,600 mi. (2,560 km) of the mid-Pacific; seven of these islands at the southeast end of the chain are inhabited. These include: Hawai'i (called the "Big Island" as it is almost twice the size of all the other islands combined), O'ahu (on which the city of Honolulu is located), Maui, Kaua'i, Moloka'i, and the two smaller islands of Lana'i and Ni'ihau. Ni'ihau is privately owned and no recent biological surveys have been permitted on that island. Also present off Maui is the small, uninhabited island of Kaho'olawe, which, until quite recently, had been used by the U.S. Navy for target practice. The tiny uninhabited islets and coral atolls to the northwest of the main island grouping are locally known as the Leewards or Northwestern Hawaiian Islands. The Leewards have been designated as a federal wildlife sanctuary and seabirds, Pacific Green Sea Turtles, Monk Seals, and other wildlife visit these islands to breed.

There are 28 species of reptiles and five species of amphibians which occur in the Hawaiian Islands or, in the case of the marine reptiles, in its surrounding waters. The terrestrial and semi-aquatic species in Hawai'i represent only a small sample of the variety occurring in most continental areas. The great majority of these forms have become established in Hawai'i through the agency of man, either accompanying the ancient Polynesians on their voyaging canoes or with more recent human immigrants. Only the marine reptiles — a venomous sea snake and five species of marine turtles — are known to be indigenous to (naturally occurring in) Hawai'i. All six are found over a wide area of the tropical Pacific. It is possible that one or two of the small geckos and skinks may also prove to be indigenous, but additional genetic analysis is needed before a more definitive statement can be made.

Amphibians as a group, because of their soft, moist skin, are not adapted to dispersal across saltwater and are rarely present on oceanic islands. Of the five species of frogs and toads now established on the Hawaiian Islands, four may

Tropical Beach near Akaka Falls (Big Island).

be categorized as purposely introduced with the approval of the appropriate state agencies. The fifth was a recent unauthorized introduction.

The history of the introduction of amphibians into the Hawaiian Islands is both intriguing and somewhat enigmatic. The 1855 Proceedings of the Royal Agricultural Society of Hawai'i states that no frogs or toads were present at the time and that it would be beneficial to introduce some. In the fall of 1857, botanist William Hillebrand imported large, dark frogs from California [probably Red-legged Frogs *(Rana aurora)*] and released them in a taro patch inland from Honolulu on O'ahu. However, after several months, their vocalizations were no longer heard and it was assumed they had perished (E. H. Bryan, 1932). In 1880, Captain Christiansen of the schooner Helene brought four dozen live frogs from California for his friend John Hassinger. The unidentified frogs were initially kept on Hassinger's property on Pensacola St. and later released with unknown results (E. H. Bryan, 1932). Commenting on amphibians in Hawai'i, Jordon and Everman (1905) noted that frogs were introduced prior to 1867 and in that particular year some were brought in from California and "placed in fresh water around Honolulu." Regrettably, no specific types nor sources are mentioned, nor is there any indication as to whether any of these frogs survived. Jordon and Everman (1905) do state that in

Water Reserve, Nu'uanu Reservoir (O'ahu). The reservoir and surrounding secondary growth riparian habitat is home to softshell turtles, Giant Toads, Bull-frogs, Green Iguanas, Metallic Skinks, small nocturnal geckos and Jackson's Chameleons.

October, 1879, a shipment of six dozen frogs which, from their description, can only be Bullfrogs *(Rana catesbeiana)*, were brought by ship in a barrel from Contra Costa County in northern California. These were released in "various places around Hilo (on the Big Island) where they soon became abundant" and offspring were soon transferred to other islands. However, Jennings and Hayes (1985) believe the 1879 date to be in error and that the actual date of introduction was October, 1897. Still another early reference lists the date of entry for the Bullfrog into the Hawaiian Islands as 1899.

During the 1890s, Albert Koebele, an entomologist employed by the Republic of Hawai'i to control pest species of insects, brought back frogs and toads from Japan and California. In an 1897 year-end report, he specifically states that "toads from California and Japan are breeding and the four species of Japanese frogs [are] no doubt as well." While Koebele does not name the individual species by name, it is probable that two of the four Japanese frogs were the Wrinkled Frog *(Rana rugosa)* and the Black-spotted Frog *(Rana nigromaculata)*. The toad species from California was most likely the California Toad *(Bufo boreas halophilus)*, possibly misidentified by E. H. Bryan (1932) as the American Toad *(Bufo americanus)*. In 1899, Koebele also tried introducing salamanders (of unidentified species) onto O'ahu, but none survived (E. H. Bryan, 1932). It is reported by W. A. Bryan (1915) that tadpoles of

Stream Valley, Manoa Stream (O'ahu). Areas such as this one are utilized by Bullfrogs, Wrinkled Frogs, Green and Black Dart-Poison Frogs, Giant Toads, Metallic Skinks, Moth Skinks, all small nocturnal gecko species and Jackson's Chameleons.

various species of frogs and toads are plentiful [on O'ahu] in the pools along the streams far up into the mountains."

Another amphibian, the Asiatic Toad *(Bufo bufo)*, was recorded by Svihla (1936) and Tinker (1938) from a single specimen found by Alfred Duvell on Kaua'i. The Black-spotted Frog was reported from O'ahu by Tinker (1938). Neither the California Toad, the Asiatic Toad, nor the Black-spotted Frog are part of the current herpetofauna. However, the Black-spotted Frog was well established on the Honolulu side of O'ahu for over half a century in streams and taro patches slightly inland from the present site of the Ala Moana Center (Tinker, pers. com.) and in Waipahu. The urban spread of Honolulu is primarily responsible for its disappearance. The last specimen seen on O'ahu was in the early 1950s (Tinker, pers. com.).

In addition to the American Toad *(Bufo americanus)*, E. H. Bryan (1932) lists the Leopard Frog *(Rana pipiens)* as being introduced on O'ahu. However, Bryan (1932; pers. com., 1977) had no additional data on the introduction or status of these two species. Neither should be considered to have become established in Hawai'i. Tinker (1938) also listed the Green Frog *(Rana clamitans)*

Suburban backyard (Oʻahu). A well-planted yard like this one on Oʻahu may support Giant Toads, all species of nocturnal and diurnal geckos, Metallic Skinks, Moth Skinks as well as all anoles occurring in the Islands.

as present. However, these later proved to be misidentified Bullfrogs *(Rana catesbeiana)* (Tinker, pers. com.). Both E. H. Bryan (1932) and Tinker (1938) documented that E. M. Ehrhorn introduced about 25 Green and Golden Bell Frogs *(Litoria aurea)* from Australia into three locations on Oʻahu in 1929. They stated that these do not appear to have survived. None of the four species mentioned in this paragraph — the American Toad, the Leopard Frog, the Green Frog and the Green and Golden Bell Frog — is part of the current herpetofauna.

Amphibian introductions during the 1930s were more successful. In 1932, at the request of the Hawaiian Sugar Planters' Association, C. E. Pemberton brought in 148 adult Giant Toads *(Bufo marinus)* from Puerto Rico to feed on sugarcane beetles. He reported a mere two years later that their numbers on Oʻahu had swelled to over 100,000. Some of these were released by Pemberton onto the other main Hawaiian Islands as well. Also in 1932, David T. Fullway, an entomologist with the Territory of Hawaiʻi, brought back 206 Green and Black Dart-Poison Frogs *(Dendrobates auratus)*. These were collected on either Toboga or Tobogilla Island in the Gulf of Panama. They were released in Upper Manoa Valley on Oʻahu for mosquito control. These frogs have since spread to a few other moist valleys on both sides of the Koʻolau range, but their distribution remains limited and they have not become established on neighboring islands. During the 1980s, Cuban Treefrogs *(Osteopilus*

Partially disturbed native forest, Upper Manoa Valley (O'ahu). Both density of individuals and total number of species of amphibians and reptiles are reduced in areas of native forest. This habitat is marginally utilized by Metallic Skinks and small nocturnal geckos.

septentrionalis) were released by a misguided hobbyist on O'ahu and this species is now also established.

Seven species of lizards, including four geckos — the Mourning Gecko *(Lepidodactylus lugubris)*, the Stump-toed Gecko *(Gehyra mutilata)*, the Tree Gecko *(Hemiphyllodactylus typus)* and the Indo-Pacific Gecko *(Hemidactylus garnotii)* — as well as three skinks — the Moth Skink *(Lipinia n. noctua)*, the Snake-eyed Skink *(Cryptoblepharus poecilopleurus)*, and the Azure-tailed Skink *(Emoia impar)* — were probably present in Hawai'i before the arrival of Captain James Cook and the first Europeans. Because of the wide dispersal of all of these lizards on Pacific islands and because of their morphological uniformity throughout their range, it is possible that most, if not all, were unintentionally transported on a number of occasions to the Hawaiian Islands by the early Polynesians in their double-hulled voyaging canoes. However, for several species, rafting on floating debris cannot be entirely ruled out. Many geckos and skinks are superior rafters and stowaways. Geckos can hide almost anywhere and their eggs have an unusually hard, durable shell that can stand up to adverse conditions. Skinks, because of their streamlined shape and burrowing nature, have the ability to get under or inside wood and other material and in this way, protect themselves from both detection and external hazards.

Fern forest, Volcanoes National Park (Big Island). Cool nighttime temperatures at areas of high elevation on Maui and the Big Island preclude non-montane adapted amphibians and reptiles from being present. It is likely that Jackson's Chameleons will move into these areas as their range on both islands continues to expand.

What is now the most common species of gecko in the islands, the House Gecko *(Hemidactylus frenatus)*, is believed to have entered Hawai'i as a stowaway aboard equipment moved between Pacific islands during or just following World War II. The presence of two skinks, the Metallic Skink *(Lampropholis delicata)* and the Copper-tailed Skink *(Emoia cyanura)*, is more enigmatic. The Metallic Skink, first recorded in 1909, is small, generalized and a potentially good stowaway. It is largely absent from the islands of Polynesia and is instead native to eastern Australia, more than 3,000 mi. (4,830 km) away. Perhaps this lizard arrived aboard a shipping vessel bringing wood or plant imports. While its origins and date of entry are in doubt, today it is the most common species of skink on all the major Hawaiian Islands. The second species, the Copper-tailed Skink *(Emoia cyanura)*, has only been found in a single, small area on the island of Kaua'i. It may represent an accidental introduction from Fiji or elsewhere in the South Pacific during the 20th Century, or it may be a species that arrived with the early Hawaiians, and remained unknown to science until 1979.

The remaining, more recently established lizards include: one iguanid, three anoles, three geckos and one Old World chameleon. The first of these is the

Green Anole *(Anolis carolinensis)*. First brought to the attention of Paul Breese, former Director of the Honolulu Zoo, in the Kaimuki district of Honolulu on O'ahu in 1950, it now occurs on all of the main islands. As the initial diurnal lizard living in vegetation around human dwellings, it was a "natural" to become established.

Another species of lizard that is thoroughly established on O'ahu is the Green Iguana *(Iguana iguana)*, a native of Mexico and central and northern South America. Wild specimens, probably escaped pets, were reported to the State Department of Agriculture beginning in the 1950s. By the 1960s, reproductive populations were established in Nu'uanu and Manoa Valleys and can now be found in several other locations on O'ahu as well. This is a low-density species on O'ahu. Although individual specimens are occasionally sighted on Kaua'i, Maui and the Big Island of Hawai'i, it does not appear, as yet, to be established outside O'ahu.

Two horned lizards, the Texas Horned Lizard *(Phrynosoma cornutum)* and the Coast Horned Lizard *(Phrynosoma coronatum),* were released in the Hawaiian Islands. The first of these was the Coast Horned Lizard which was brought in some numbers to O'ahu in the 1890s and the first decade of the 20th century (Jennings, 1987). The Texas Horned lizard was reported by Hunsaker and Breese (1967) to be an established species at two locations on O'ahu during the 1960s. It was available in several Island pet shops during this period. While this horned lizard apparently survived in the wild for one or more generations, it had, by the late 1970s, died out. The relatively high humidity level throughout O'ahu combined with the presence of rats, mongooses and feral cats may , in part, be responsible for its failure to establish a sustaining wild population.

One of the most unusual reptiles to become established in the Hawaiian Islands is the remarkable Jackson's Chameleon *(Chamaeleo jacksonii xantholophus)*. This is a true Old World chameleon from East Africa with turreted eyes, a retractable, pistol-like tongue and, of course, the ability to vary its color. This lizard was imported by a pet shop owner on windward O'ahu and a number were released by him in 1972 in Kane'ohe to which they readily adapted and began reproducing. By 1980, there were five different populations of these lizards occurring on windward O'ahu. During the 1980s, many were collected as backyard pets by local residents. By the mid 1990s, this species was well established on both sides of O'ahu as well as on Maui and the Big Island. In 1995, the first small breeding populations were recorded in the wild from Kaua'i and the first specimens were documented on Lana'i.

Several other lizards have become established in Hawai'i subsequent to 1978 when the first edition of this book, *Hawaiian Reptiles and Amphibians,* was published. One of these, the Tokay Gecko *(Gekko gecko),* is from southeast Asia. A few individual lizards first appeared during the late 1960s and early 1970s. These were possibly brought back as pets by servicemen stationed overseas in southeast Asia during the Vietnam War. Breeding populations on Oʻahu were initially brought to the attention of the author in 1980 and 1981. Two other geckos are now established in Hawaiʻi as well. The Gold Dust Day Gecko *(Phelsuma l. laticauda),* was brought in and released by a University of Hawaiʻi student in 1974 in upper Manoa Valley. It took about five years for the population to expand to where it was brought to the attention of island herpetologists. This species is now widely distributed on Oʻahu and the Big Island. It is present on Maui as well. The Orange-spotted Day Gecko *(Phelsuma g. guimbeaui)* first appeared in the early 1980s when it was briefly available in the exotic pet trade and is believed to have descended from escaped pets of a hobbyist. Breeding populations are present in Kaneʻohe, the Makiki district of Honolulu and Kailua on Oʻahu. Two anoles became established during the 1980s. These are the Brown Anole *(Anolis sagrei)* and the Knight Anole *(Anolis equestris).* Both are species that were earlier introduced into Florida and are common in the exotic pet trade there. It is thought that these species may have been brought in as children's pets from Florida in the early 1980s. Breeding populations of Knight Anoles exist both in Kaneʻohe and in the Lanikai area on windward Oʻahu. The Brown Anole is distributed in a number of disjunct populations on the windward side of that island and in Waikiki.

The only land snake established in the wild in Hawaiʻi is the tiny secretive Island Blind Snake *(Ramphotyphlops braminus).* This reptile, an expert stowaway, is believed to have been introduced unintentionally from the Philippines amidst soil surrounding a large shipment of plants used in landscaping the campus of Kamehameha Schools in Honolulu. It was first recorded in 1930 and is now present throughout Oʻahu and on all the other main islands.

The one snake species highly injurious to island ecosystems, the Brown Tree Snake *(Boiga irregularis),* is **not**, at the time of this writing, established in the Hawaiian Islands. A very limited number of Brown Tree Snakes have turned up in Hawaiʻi, either on the flight line near military aircraft or other aircraft from Guam, in the plane itself, or in military storage warehouses on Oʻahu where cargo from Guam is stored. Great effort is being made to keep these snakes from leaving Guam in planes and boats as well as to prevent their possible dispersal upon arrival in the Hawaiian Islands. A special section in this book discusses the Brown Tree Snake and these efforts in some detail. It will also help familiarize the reader with the danger presented by "island supertramp" (highly injurious, non-native, easily dispersed) species of animals to Hawaiian ecosystems.

A freshwater chelonian, the Chinese Softshell Turtle *(Pelodiscus sinensis),* reported by Brock (1947), was imported from the Orient alive on a number of occasions as a food item, perhaps as early as the mid- to late 1800s. The Chinese Softshell is the less common of the two softshell species in Kauaʻi and Oʻahu. A somewhat similar appearing Asian species, the Wattle-necked Softshell Turtle *(Palea steindachneri)* is more widely distributed in suitable aquatic habitats on both Oʻahu and Kauaʻi. The wild, reproducing populations on these islands are descendants of both purposely released and escaped fish pond stock (McKeown and Webb, 1982). Both species were also brought into Hawaiʻi alive as food items. A number of releases may have occurred between the mid-1800s and 1942 when importation, due to the outbreak of World War II, ceased for both species. Another turtle, the Red-eared Slider *(Trachemys scripta elegans)*, entered the Hawaiian Islands through the pet trade. Commonly sold in pet shops in the Islands for a number of decades, released and escaped individuals were turning up in waterways on Oʻahu and Kauaʻi in the 1970s. By the early 1980s, the population in the large freshwater area comprising the Kawai Nui Marsh and surrounding drainage ditches, inland from Kailua, Oʻahu were regularly producing offspring.

In summary, of the thirty-three species of reptiles and amphibians now established in the Hawaiian Islands, only five marine turtles and one venomous sea snake are known to be indigenous. All the others, like Hawaiʻi's diverse human population, are relatively recent immigrants.

Although few non-native animals can be considered completely benign with respect to endemic island ecosystems, the majority of the introduced amphibian and reptile species in the Hawaiian Islands live in vegetation around human dwellings or in disturbed habitat in association with both alien plant and insect species. These herptiles provide a useful service by helping to control the non-native invertebrates occurring in these areas. In this regard, as well as in color and form, they may be appreciated along with the beautiful introduced plants found in yards and gardens in Hawaiʻi.

Gold Dust Day Gecko, *Phelsuma laticauda laticauda*. A beneficial introduced lizard that resides in vegetation around human dwellings.

AMPHIBIANS
CLASS AMPHIBIA

Introduction

Amphibians as a group are an ancient class of vertebrate animals. Fossil skeletons have been dated from the Devonian Period, 370 million years ago. The word "amphibian" is derived from the Greek *amphi* meaning "both" or "double" and *bios,* meaning "life." There are over 4,500 living species in the Class Amphibia. They are divided among three orders: the frogs and toads (Order Anura), with just under 4,000 species; the salamanders (Order Caudata) containing approximately 400 species; and the tropical legless caecilians (Order Gymnophiona) with about 160 species.

Relation to Other Vertebrates

Amphibians are ectothermic ("cold-blooded") vertebrates that stand intermediate on the evolutionary scale between the aquatic fish and the primarily terrestrial reptiles. Amphibians have soft, moist, smooth or warty skin liberally supplied with mucous glands. Because the skin is thin and somewhat porous, most amphibians are poorly adapted to living exclusively on land. They must never venture too far from water or cool, damp places because their skin is in constant danger of drying out. Normal moisture loss is replaced through skin absorption.

Life History

The amphibian life cycle begins with the fertilized egg. The jelly-coated eggs are typically laid in a moist environment which decreases their chances of drying out. The eggs develop into larvae which breathe through gills and live out the first stage of their lives in water. The surviving larvae characteristically undergo a metamorphosis which prepares them for the second stage of life on land. The cycle is completed when the adult returns to the water to breed. There are, however, exceptions to the characteristic life cycle — a few frogs, toads and many salamanders bypass the larval stage altogether and emerge from the egg in miniature adult-like form.

Many amphibians are useful in controlling the number of noxious insects and other invertebrate pests. The compounds in the skin toxins produced by some toads and dart-poison frogs are just starting to be more widely utilized in human medicine.

Of the three orders of amphibians, only the frogs and toads occur in the wild in the Hawaiian Islands.

FROGS AND TOADS
Order Anura

Frogs and toads (anurans) are easily recognizable to most people. Typically, as adults, they have short, fat bodies, slim waists, and no tail. All have four legs, generally with four toes on each of the front feet and five on each of the hind feet. The rear legs are usually well-developed for hopping or jumping, with webbing between the toes. All frogs and toads, as adults, are carnivorous. Each has a sticky tongue that is attached to the front of the mouth. A specific movement or series of movements by potential prey triggers a feeding response. The frog's mouth opens and the tongue is rapidly flicked forward to catch the unsuspecting insect or other prey item.

While virtually all species of frogs and toads can vocalize, it is usually only the males that do the calling. During periods of courtship and mating, these calls draw both sexes together in an aquatic environment for egg-laying and amplexus. During amplexus, the male embraces the female from behind. Typically, as the eggs are laid, the male discharges sperm so that the eggs are actually fertilized in the water or other moist place outside of the female's body. The number of eggs laid may range from a few to several thousand. Courtship and reproductive strategies vary from species to species.

Eggs from five anuran species occurring on the Hawaiian Islands develop into larval forms commonly known as tadpoles. Tadpoles breathe through gills, have mouth parts adapted for scraping, and may be either herbivorous (eating plant material), omnivorous (eating plant material and animal material), or carnivorous (eating only animal material). Through a gradual metamorphosis in which the gills and tail are reabsorbed and limbs are grown, anuran tadpoles transform into adult form and grow to breeding size over a period ranging from a number of months to several years, depending on the species. Adult frogs and toads breathe air through lungs in addition to skin respiration. As adults, they feed on insects and other small animals.

Herpetologists are occasionally asked, "What is the difference between a frog and a toad?" Typically, frogs have smooth skin, well-developed hind legs and live in or around water. Toads, on the other hand, have rough, wart-like skin, shorter hind legs and, as adults, live primarily on land. On a worldwide basis, the terms "frog" and "toad" do not accurately describe the majority of the world's anurans which are classified into 21 or more additional families: some frog-like, some toad-like, and many with characteristics all their own. For these reasons, the vernacular name "frog" may be used for **all** members of the order.

There are species from four major families of frogs that have been successfully introduced into the Hawaiian Islands. These four families are the dart-poison frogs (Dendrobatidae), the true frogs (Ranidae), true toads (Bufonidae) and the treefrogs (Hylidae).

DART-POISON FROGS
Family Dendrobatidae

Dart-poison frogs, or poison-arrow frogs as they are sometimes called, are tiny, active, brightly colored anurans from the tropical rainforests of Central and South America. There are approximately 160 different species. All, for which there is data, have well-developed courtship and parental care. Their eggs are laid in small numbers in the leaf joints of epiphytic plants such as bromeliads, or in moist, protected locations on land and are typically "guarded" by one of the parents. The name "dart-poison frog" is applied to members of this family because some of the indigenous Native American peoples from these areas traditionally apply the concentrated, highly toxic, alkaloid skin secretions from a few species of these frogs to the tips of their blow gun darts. When the darts are shot into a small or mid-sized animal and the poison enters the bloodstream, it is effective in bringing down the intended prey. However, almost all dart-poison frogs, including the species introduced into Hawai'i, are *not* dangerous to handle in a normal manner. Nevertheless, as a matter of common sense, wash your hands after touching one of these amphibians to rinse away any residual toxins that might be present.

Green and Black Dart-Poison Frog
(Dendrobates auratus)

Green and Black Dart-Poison Frog, *Dendrobates auratus.*

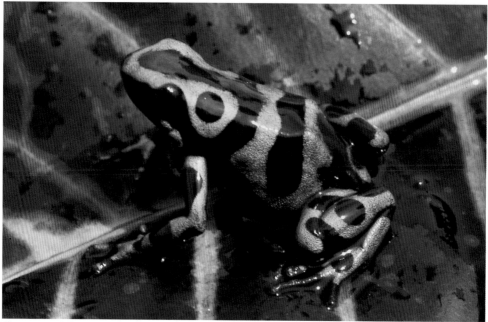

Green and Black Dart-Poison Frog on croton leaf.

The Green and Black Dart-Poison Frog was purposely introduced into Hawai'i by David T. Fullway, an entomologist employed by the Territory of Hawai'i to bring in beneficial animals to eat non-native insects. Two hundred and six initial specimens were collected from either Toboga or Tobagilla Island off the Pacific coast of Panama in 1932. These were released into upper Manoa Valley on O'ahu to assist in mosquito control.

This vividly patterned green and black frog, the size of a 25-cent-piece, is the island's most strikingly marked amphibian. The brilliant markings it possesses are referred to as "warning colors" and serve to alert potential predators that this frog may be poisonous, if eaten. The skin toxins, however, are not dangerous to humans unless swallowed or rubbed into the eyes or other mucous membrane areas. These frogs are most active during or just after rains. On sunny days, they are less active. They may be encountered on cloudy days in the early morning and late afternoon, when the rays of the sun do not shine down so intensely onto the sheltered valley areas that they typically inhabit. These beautiful little frogs move with a jerky gait and hop low to the ground. During the cooler, wetter months of the year (November–April), these amphibians may

Tadpole-carrying.

Green and Black Dart-Poison Frog tadpole.

be more frequently encountered out in the open, having ventured forth in search of mosquitos and other small insects. However, during late spring, summer and early fall, these frogs are relatively inactive, staying close to moist places such as under debris, logs, stones, in the tangled root systems of trees or under elevated valley homes. They almost never enter streams but occasionally frequent shallow pools of standing water in such places as depressions in lava rocks, or amidst or under rainwater-filled debris.

The Green and Black Dart-Poison Frog has well-developed courtship behavior. The male will usually call to attract a female. If more than one male or more than one female with ripe eggs hops into the area, ritualized combat between individuals of the same sex usually occurs. Individuals square off, push and shove each other, sometimes standing on their hind legs, in a manner reminiscent of human sumo wrestlers. The winning frog earns the right to accompany its

Typical habitat of the Green and Black Dart-Poison Frog.

prospective mate to a protected, secluded location nearby. Instead of amplexus occurring, the female deposits her eggs in a moist, sheltered place on land where they are fertilized by the male. The male returns to the "nest" site from time to time to tend or "guard" the eggs. About two weeks later, when the eggs hatch, one of the parents, usually the male, transports the emerging tadpoles to nearby standing water by allowing them to "swim" onto its back. Later, the parent may "tadpole-carry" both small and large tadpoles on its back between available suitable standing water sources. The tadpoles of this particular species are omnivorous with a carnivorous emphasis, feeding on live mosquito larvae, daphnia, drowned insects, as well as algae and moss. Tadpoles grow to about $7/8$ in. (22 mm) although individual Green and Black Dart-Poison Frog tadpoles as large as $1^3/4$ in. (45 mm) have been recorded in Hawai'i.

Identification: Quite distinctive, adults are typically black or deep chocolate brown with large green or greenish-yellow spots or bars over the entire body. Substantial color variation exists within Hawaiian populations, with individuals possessing a variety of markings, as these randomly photographed individuals in this book show. Very rarely, Hawaiian specimens will lack green pigment and will be a black and white color, or even purple and white, as one of the illustrations demonstrates.

There is little, if any, obvious sexual dimorphism. Fully adult females may be slightly larger and, if gravid, slightly more robust than males. The sexes are most accurately told apart by behavior. Only the males vocalize. During calling, the vocal sac of the male is inflated. Calling serves to announce the male's presence to females and to signal other males not to enter his territory.

Distribution: The Green and Black Dart-Poison Frog occurs in only a few well-foliated, moist valleys on leeward and windward O'ahu. It is native to Central America. These beautiful frogs are highly sensitive to destruction of their habitat on O'ahu as well as over-collection. It is best to observe and photograph, but not to collect this interesting species.

Interesting Fact: Another good reason **not** to collect these frogs from the wild in large numbers is that newly wild-caught specimens produce skin toxins that can poison other frogs of their own species, *particularly* if they are housed more than 3 or 4 to a 10-gallon (38 liter) terrarium or if the enclosure is not thoroughly rinsed on a daily basis. Wild-caught dart-poison frogs affected by skin toxins will show signs of paralysis, followed by death. Interestingly, captive-bred dart-poison frogs typically lack these alkaloid skin toxins and no such problems are encountered with captive-bred specimens.

Care in Captivity: These amphibians are only appropriate to be kept in captivity by individuals with *advanced* skills in maintaining amphibians in tropical, planted vivaria with drip/misting systems which simulate natural rainfall. They are not suitable for the beginning hobbyist nor as a pet shop animal. If not properly maintained, they will soon die.

Green and Black Dart-Poison Frog, *Dendrobates auratus,* subadult. Green color is not present on juveniles and only begins to appear as the frog develops into a subadult.

Dart-poison frogs are excellent climbers. As captives, they need to be housed in secure terraria, such as those with sliding screen tops with latching doors or set pins. Live potted plants, such as bromeliads and orchids need to be included along with a shallow dish of water that the frogs can enter. Adult frogs must be fed daily. In Hawai'i, placing a few chicken bones on a flat plate near a trail of ants will produce large numbers of ants. These can be shaken into a clear plastic bag or plastic jar to which vitamin-mineral powder has just been added. Next, empty the ants into a flat petri dish at the bottom of the terrarium. Each adult frog will take from 40

Green and Black Dart-Poison Frog lacking green pigment.

Green and Black Dart-Poison Frog, gravid female.

to 70 small black (Argentine) ants per daily feeding. On the U.S. mainland, wingless fruit flies *(Drosophila)*, which can be raised in canning jars using medium purchased from biological supply houses, and hatchling crickets, available from invertebrate suppliers, are the preferred dietary fare. All insects must be "dusted," that is, lightly coated with a powdered vitamin/mineral supplement for proper nutrition. Tadpoles of this species should be housed individually in separate container and fed high-protein Tetra® breeder fish food flakes and chopped tubifex worms. The water for tadpoles should either be on a filtration system or cleaned or replaced daily. Tap water, in cities where water is treated with chlorine, should be set out in an open container for 24 hours before it is used in either adult or tadpole dart-poison frog enclosures.

An alternate method of raising dart-poison frog tadpoles in Hawai'i for the advanced hobbyist is to raise them collectively, in a child's plastic swimming pool partially filled with non-chlorinated water. When housed in groups, it is essential that large amounts of potential food, such as live daphnia be present in the enclosure at all times. Otherwise, the primarily carnivorous tadpoles may try to consume each other. At night, tadpoles of this species often rest just below the water surface, with their heads pointing straight up, and their tails pointing straight down.

Green and Black Dart-Poison Frog with network pattern.

Green and Black Dart-Poison Frog in rock cavity.

TREEFROGS
Family Hylidae

Treefrogs are represented by about 720 species worldwide with the greatest number occurring in the Americas, Europe and Asia. As their name implies, treefrogs are specially adapted for climbing. As adults, they have well-developed legs with especially long rear limbs. The toes on each foot end with an adhesive toe pad. These frogs have slim waists. They not only climb well, but can also generally hop a considerable distance, if disturbed. Interestingly, only a few species live high in trees. The majority live in low vegetation in woodlands or wetlands. Some may prefer resting on rocks, trunks of trees or in or on hollow logs. When in a resting position, the body is usually positioned compactly against the resting surface, making the frog difficult to detect by predators. Typically, these amphibians are most active at night. Many are capable of color changes, depending on such factors as activity level, time of day, as well as temperature and humidity levels. Male treefrogs have a vocal sac that can be inflated. Only the males sing.

Cuban Treefrog
(Osteopilus septentrionalis)

Cuban Treefrog.

Virtually all but a very few individual species of treefrogs would be both beneficial and benign if they were to be introduced into the Hawaiian Islands. Regrettably, the single species that has the capacity to do great harm to island ecosystems, the Cuban Treefrog, is now present in Hawai'i.

Cuban Treefrog.

The Cuban Treefrog is an island supertramp species which is capable of living in very high densities in natural areas as well as suburban neighborhoods. Cuban Treefrogs are highly predaceous with a broad diet. They will eat almost any type of animal they can fit into their large mouths including native and introduced insects, other invertebrates, any frog or toad smaller than themselves, lizards, and possibly even small birds. These frogs are efficient predators.

Cuban Treefrog.

They have tremendous mobility as well as the ability to thrive in a variety of habitats from sea level to over 3,000 ft. (900 m). Thus, they could represent a potential ecological nightmare. In the author's opinion, every effort must be made to eradicate this species from the island of O'ahu before its range significantly expands to a greater area of this island and to neighboring islands in the Hawaiian chain.

This recent immigrant to Hawai'i from the West Indies is one of the largest species of treefrog found anywhere in the world. During the day, these frogs are inactive, resting in protected spots with high humidity, such as in the leaf joints of palms and other plants, in yard shrubbery, on rocks near ponds or streams, or under elevated houses. At night they are active in search of prey. The Cuban treefrog is capable of rapid color change and exhibits a high degree of both color and pattern variation. Individuals may be cream-colored, brown, light gray, bronze, green or any combination of these hues. The dorsum is usually mottled and the flank areas are often yellow. Unlike most other treefrogs, the skin of the Cuban Treefrog is slightly warty and, if handled, the skin secretions can be irritating if not washed off.

Male Cuban Treefrogs vocalize at night or sometimes, during the day, just after it rains. When calling, the partially divided vocal sac inflates outward. The call has been described as a high-pitched "rasping, snore-like noise" and as a "grating squawk."

Identification: Toe pad discs on both the front and back feet are greatly expanded. Males are $1^1/_2$–$3^1/_2$ in. (38–85 mm) while females average $2^1/_2$–4 in. (6.4–10.2 cm) in snout-vent length. In Florida, females up to $6^1/_4$ in. (16.5 cm) have been recorded. Females are longer lived than males with a potential life span of two to five years or longer. Males typically only live for one to two years. Cuban Treefrog tadpoles grow to a length of $1^1/_{16}$–$1^1/_4$ in. (26–32 mm) before metamorphosis. Tadpoles may be distinguished from those of the Giant Toad by their slightly different shape and their ability to grow to a larger size.

Reproduction: Cuban Treefrogs are capable of breeding in Hawai'i virtually throughout the year. Greatest breeding activity is during the wetter months. Males call to attract females. Gravid females are opportunistic in regard to their laying site. As amplexus occurs, eggs are laid in ponds, marshes, drainage ditches or almost any available standing water source.

Distribution: Native to Cuba, the Bahamas, the Cayman Islands and previously introduced into Puerto Rico and St. Croix, Hawaiian specimens appear to have been illegally imported in the early 1980s from southern Florida. Cuban Treefrogs became established in Florida prior to 1931 and are now commonly sold there through the exotic pet trade. At the time of publication, Cuban Treefrogs were restricted to the Ko'olau mountain watershed and the area inland from Kane'ohe on O'ahu.

Cuban Treefrog metamorphosing. Note the tail is beginning to be absorbed.

Interesting Facts: Because of its ecosystem-damaging propensities, this frog is inappropriate as a pet species in Hawai'i. In fact, although it is a long-shot that it can be eliminated from O'ahu at this point, it is still worth trying. Adults should be humanely euthanized or turned over to the State Department of Agriculture. Large predaceous fish,

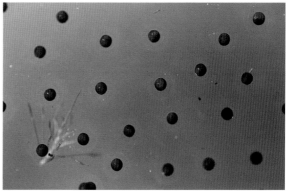

Cuban Treefrog eggs.

such as cichlids, may be effective at consuming Cuban Treefrog tadpoles in breeding ponds. Additional control of tadpoles at breeding sites by the State Department of Agriculture or other appropriate governmental agency may be warranted.

TRUE FROGS
Family Ranidae

True frogs are a diverse group and are represented worldwide by over 625 species. Many live in or around rivers, lakes, and streams. Typically, they are long-legged, narrow-waisted, and smooth-skinned. Most have substantial webbing between their rear toes and are prodigious leapers when escaping from danger.

Bullfrog
(Rana catesbeiana)
Hawaiian name: Poloka Iana

Bullfrog.

The Bullfrog is the largest frog native to the continental United States. It is semiaquatic and may be found along the banks of or in large slow-moving streams, rivers, ponds, marshes, and reservoirs. This frog feeds on almost anything that moves which is small enough to stuff into its mouth. Prey consists of a wide variety of terrestrial and aquatic insects and other invertebrates. These include, but are not limited to: crayfish, crickets, grasshoppers, cockroaches, worms, snails and slugs. Vertebrate prey include fishes, other frogs, mice and even baby water birds.

Bullfrog tadpole.

This frog is one of the first amphibians to become successfully established in Hawai'i. Initially, it was purposely introduced from Contra Costa County in northern California to the Hilo area of the Big Island in either 1879, 1897, or 1899, depending on the literature source. It was brought to the Islands as a food source and to consume harmful, introduced aquatic invertebrates. Frog

Bullfrog color variant. Note the tympanum on the female is about the size of the eye.

Bullfrog. Note enlarged tympanum present on male.

legs were documented as being available in local marketplaces in Hawai'i as early as 1900.

The Bullfrog is an excellent swimmer and jumper. A large individual is capable of jumping 6 ft. (2 m) or more on a single leap. This amphibian is frequently encountered along the water's edge and, if disturbed, makes a characteristic squawking noise, followed by a loud splash, as it jumps into the water and frog-kicks to the bottom.

Bullfrogs are an "island supertramp" species that can live in and around almost any freshwater source and will eat almost anything smaller than themselves. As such, this particular amphibian is well-suited to be managed as a game species. Despite their wide distribution in the Hawaiian Islands, these frogs should NEVER be introduced into any water source in the islands in which they do not already occur, as their feeding habits can cause damage to native, aquatic organisms and to Wrinkled Frogs.

Bullfrog, ventral view. Note extensive webbing between rear toes.

Identification: Bullfrogs average 4–7 in. (10–17 cm); record 8 in. (20.3 cm) in snout-vent length. They have smooth skin and are mottled brown, typically with a green snout. Throats on males are often yellow. The underside of the body is whitish with dark spotting. The eardrum (tympanum) of the male is larger in size than the frog's eye. In females and juveniles, the eardrum approximates the size of the eye. The Bullfrog may be distinguished from the Giant Toad by the *absence* of both warts and enlarged parotoid glands on the sides of the neck. Bullfrogs lack dorsal ridges that are present in Wrinkled Frogs and are quickly differentiated from Cuban Treefrogs by the absence of toe pads. Bullfrog tadpoles are olive-green above with black spotting and whitish or pale yellow below.

Reproduction: Bullfrogs are most active at night. Males stake out territories in the water and bellow to attract females. During amplexus, the female releases her eggs which are fertilized externally by the male as they leave the female's cloaca. Eggs of Bullfrogs are laid in round egg masses up to 1 ft. (30 cm) across, among plants on the water's surface. The tadpoles grow to be 3–5 in. (7.5–12.5 cm) in length. However, because of Hawai'i's subtropical climate, they typically transform into frogs in less than six months instead of the usual two years.

Distribution: The Bullfrog occurs on all the main Hawaiian Islands where aquatic habitat exists. These frogs were more common in the state of Hawai'i 50 to 75 years ago before many lowland taro patches and freshwater marshes were drained to make way for urbanization. It is native to the eastern and central United States but has been widely transported by humans throughout the world as a food source.

Interesting Fact: Bullfrogs are not native to the American West, including California, from which they were initially brought to the Hawaiian Islands. Several of the introductions of Bullfrogs into different parts of California in the early 1900s were actually of Hawaiian Bullfrogs with California "roots."

Care in Captivity: The tadpoles are ideal for keeping indoors in a classroom by teachers. They will feed on aquatic plants, algae and tropical fish food and must have food present or be offered food daily. Newly transformed froglets will take crickets, grasshoppers or earthworms. Adults can become too large for indoor maintenance and are best housed in an outdoor enclosure with a pond. Adults will eat any invertebrate or vertebrate animal smaller than itself including laboratory mice. Adult frogs will also take dog and cat food in a food dish if earthworms or mealworms are added, at least initially, to simulate prey movement. Newly metamorphosed frogs should be offered food three times a week and adults about twice a week.

Wrinkled Frog
(*Rana rugosa*)

The Wrinkled Frog was purposely brought to Hawai'i from Japan in 1895 or early 1896 by Albert Koebele, an entomologist working for the Republic of Hawai'i, to help control introduced insects. It has since become established in mountain streams which offer both abundant shade and year-round, clear, cool, running water. These amphibians like to bask on rocks protruding out of the stream or along the stream bank. Where this frog coinhabits some of the larger streams with the Bullfrog, the latter typically lives in the broader, deeper sections. The Wrinkled Frog is found in shallow pools, generally further upstream, where Bullfrogs are either absent or in small numbers. These species are rarely encountered together as the Bullfrog is an aggressive feeder and will consume almost anything smaller than itself, including Wrinkled Frogs.

A good leaper, if alarmed, the Wrinkled Frog will dive into the water and frog-kick to the bottom. It may hide in the leaf litter for five or ten minutes before resurfacing at a different spot.

Identification: Adult Wrinkled Frogs have an average snout-vent length of $1^1/_4$–$1^3/_4$ in. (32–44 mm). They are uniformly gray or grayish-brown, *not* mottled brown with a green head like the Bullfrog. Unlike the Giant Toad, Wrinkled Frogs lack warty skin as well as enlarged parotoid glands at the back of the head. They do not have toe pads as do Cuban Treefrogs. Tadpoles of Wrinkled Frogs resemble those of the Bullfrog but are smaller and have very little or no black spotting on the head and tail.

Metamorphosing Wrinkled Frog.

Reproduction: During amplexus, the female Wrinkled Frog lays her eggs in a jelly-like mass in slow-moving water amidst protruding sticks and vegetation. The greenish-gray tadpoles grow to about $1\frac{1}{2}$–2 in. (38–51 mm) before metamorphosing into tiny frogs that, except for size, resemble the adults.

Wrinkled Frog tadpole.

Distribution: Native to Japan and the Korean Peninsula, the Wrinkled Frog is found in suitable stream habitat in localized areas at low and mid-elevations in Hawai'i on O'ahu, the Big Island, Maui and Kaua'i.

Interesting Fact: About the size of a silver dollar and uniform charcoal or brownish-gray in color, the frog derives its common name from narrow ridges along the dorsal surface which gives its skin a "wrinkled" appearance. This amphibian is an island treasure. Except for Hawai'i, it does not appear to be established anywhere outside of its native range in Asia. A "kamaaina" resident, it does *not* negatively impact endemic species of Hawaiian insects to any degree.

Care in Captivity: As is the case for the Green and Black Dart-Poison Frog, this species is only appropriate for the advanced herpetoculturist. Wrinkled Frogs should not be collected for the pet trade as suitable habitat in Hawai'i is limited and populations of Wrinkled Frogs can be easily damaged. Wrinkled Frog tadpoles require an aquarium with an undergravel filter and live aquatic plants with algal growth on which to feed. Additionally, their diet should be supplemented with small amounts of flake fish food. Newly transformed captive froglets require two to three week-old (second and third stage) crickets or clusters of live tubifex worms which are available from most large pet shops. Adults need a well-planted vivarium which has a pool. Adult frogs will eat live crickets, earthworms, small grasshoppers, moths, some smaller forms of cockroaches, and other appropriate-sized invertebrates. In captivity, adults should be offered insect prey on an every-other-day basis.

TRUE TOADS
Family Bufonidae

   True toads are fat-bodied, warty amphibians with rough, relatively thick, dry skin. They rely on camouflage and toxic skin secretions from the parotoid glands behind the head to protect themselves from predators. Most are nocturnal and, as adults, are more terrestrial than aquatic. Toads have shorter hind legs than most other types of frogs. Instead of jumping long distances, they move in short, quick hops, or walk. They do *not* cause warts. All may be safely handled as long as it is done gently. Rough handling may result in a toad emptying its bladder. A badly treated, highly stressed toad also will produce milky-colored skin secretions which are toxic. Toads are wide-ranging amphibians found over most continental areas. Worldwide, there are about 365 species.

Giant Toad
(Bufo marinus)

Giant Toad, *Bufo marinus* in amplexus.

Hawaiian Name: Poloka

   The Giant Toad, locally called "Bufo Toad" or "Bufo," was purposely introduced into Hawai'i from Puerto Rico in 1932 by Dr. Cyril E. Pemberton, an entomologist working for the Hawaiian Sugar Planters Association. This amphibian, also known as the Giant Neotropical Toad, was obtained with the intent of controlling sugarcane beetles and other injurious insects. A total of

S. McKeown

Giant Toad, female.

148 adult toads were brought to Hawai'i. Of this group, 68 were liberated into upper Manoa Valley and 80 more were released in a taro patch near Waipio on O'ahu. The toads reproduced so rapidly that, in a little over two years, Pemberton distributed over 100,000 descendents of this stock throughout the Islands (Oliver and Shaw, 1953).

This large anuran is compact and heavy-bodied, with relatively short legs, rough, bumpy skin, and large parotoid glands on the back of the head behind the eyes. Although fond of entering water after dark, the Giant Toad is *not* dependent on water except to breed. It is capable of ranging over wide areas, effectively feeding on large quantities of cockroaches, beetles, grubs, crickets, grasshoppers, other insects, earthworms, slugs, snails, spiders and centipedes. Despite being primarily active at night, it is probably the most familiar amphibian to Hawaiian residents because it thrives in well-watered yards and gardens and is common on all the main islands.

Giant Toads occasionally eat out of dog food dishes or immerse themselves in pet water dishes to soak. However, because there are no native amphibians nor specialized wildlife that naturally feed on these toads in Hawai'i, they have not had a major negative impact in the Islands. Many residents enjoy having "Bufos" in their yards and flower beds to eat cockroaches and other noxious non-native insects and other invertebrates.

Identification: Females grow to a larger size than males, and may reach a snout-vent length of 6–7 in. (15–18 cm) or more and routinely attain a weight of over 8 oz. (23 g). Both sexes are brown, tan, or grayish in color. Huge parotoid glands and numerous large warts on the upper back readily distinguish these amphibians from Bullfrogs, Wrinkled Frogs and Cuban Treefrogs.

Reproduction: The Giant Toad breeds in fish ponds, irrigation ditches, temporary pools and reservoirs. Females are capable of producing eggs multiple times during the year. The males enter the water after sundown and begin their repetitive trilling call to attract the females. During amplexus, the male grasps the female around her chest from behind. Fertilization of the eggs is external. She releases thousands of eggs attached to one another in a string-like manner, into the water. After a few days, the eggs hatch into tiny dark-colored tadpoles. The tadpoles are herbivorous, feeding on algae and other microscopic plant life in the water. In about a month, when they are $^3/_4$ in. (22 mm) long, they are ready to undergo metamorphosis. Prior to transformation, the tadpole develops hind legs and then front legs. The mouth becomes larger and changes from a scraping form to a shape more adapted for feeding on insects. Its gills, designed for obtaining oxygen from water, develop into air-breathing lungs. As the tail is being reabsorbed, the tadpole comes to the surface of the water to breathe air. Soon, large numbers of tiny toadlets emerge onto the land. Only a few will survive to maturity and return to the water to mate as adults.

Distribution: These toads are native to southern Mexico, Central and South America. They have been widely transported by humans during the first half of the 20th century into many areas in the tropics where sugarcane is grown, despite their limited effectiveness as a sugarcane beetle predator. This species of amphibian now occurs on all of the main Hawaiian Islands.

Giant Toads are safe to gently handle as long as one's hands are washed afterwards. However, any small children must be supervised when handling toads. Rough or abusive handling will cause the toad to secrete a milky-white, cream-like, toxic fluid which can burn and even cause temporary blindness if rubbed

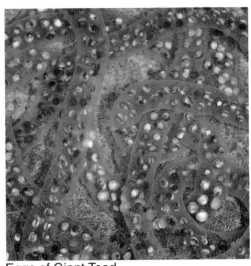

Eggs of Giant Toad.

into the eyes. Ingesting toad skin toxins can burn the mucous membranes.

A veterinarian may need to be quickly consulted if a pet dog chews on a Giant Toad which, under some circumstances if untreated, may prove fatal. Foaming from the mouth and other symptoms of distress are the most common signs of toad-chewing by a dog.

Interesting Fact: Giant Toads were introduced into Queensland, Australia from Hawai'i in 1935, also for sugarcane beetle control. In Australia, "Cane Toads," as they are called there, quickly became an "island supertramp" species, spreading through Queensland and more recently, into portions of neighboring states. Australia has many species of native frogs, but no true toads. In Australia, native predatory species of wildlife are often killed by the toxins when attempting to eat toads which they mistake for edible native frogs.

Care in Captivity: Due to their large size, adult Giant Toads do best in the garden outdoors. Subadults can be easily maintained in a large, planted, screen-topped terrarium. They need a large, shallow dish of water at one end of the

Giant Toad tadpole.

School of Giant Toad tadpoles.

enclosure. Enough insects should be offered three time a week for the toad to maintain a robust appearance. Tadpoles do best in an aquarium with a undergravel filter, live plants and overhead lighting. Algae will form on the plants in a well-lit aquarium and will be eaten by the tadpoles. Flake fish food should be added as a supplement. Live Giant Toad tadpoles are well suited for maintenance in the classroom.

REPTILES
CLASS REPTILIA

Introduction

Reptiles evolved from the amphibians. For over 150 million years, from the late Paleozoic through the entire Mesozoic Era, a truly immense period of time, dinosaurs were the dominant animal group on Earth. Within the last several years, scientists have revised their hypothesis regarding the dinosaurs. It is now considered correct to classify them more closely with the birds and the crocodilians (alligators and crocodiles). The relationship of the dinosaurs with modern reptiles is inconclusive at this time.

There are about 7,000 species of living reptiles representing four orders that are alive today. These are the alligators and crocodiles (Order Crocodylia) with about 25 species; the turtles (Order Testudines) with approximately 270 species; the amphisbaenians (tropical legless ringed lizards), lizards and snakes (Order Squamata), with over 6,300 species. In addition, two very closely related surviving members of the ancient order Rhynchocephalia, the Tuataras, exist on a number of offshore islets off New Zealand. The reptiles that occur in the wild in the Hawaiian Islands or its adjacent waters include turtles, lizards and snakes.

Relation To Other Vertebrates

Reptiles are vertebrates (backboned animals) that, like the amphibians, are ectothermic. Ectotherms derive their heat from the external environment and control their body temperature by moving between shade and sun as necessary to reach a desired internal temperature at which each prefers to be active. Reptiles have dry (not slimy) skin and have a protective covering of scales, scutes or plates. Their toes, if present, typically have claws. Reptiles were the first major group of vertebrate animals to successfully colonize the great landmasses. While some have ancient origins, others are quite modern.

Life History

Perhaps the most significant reptilian advance was the development of a "land egg" differing from those of the fish and amphibians by having a hard or flexible outer shell and extraembryonic membranes, the amnion, chorion, allantois, and yolk sac. This major evolutionary adaptation freed the reptiles from the necessity of laying their eggs in water or other moist places as well as the need of a larval stage. Not all reptiles lay eggs, however. Some lizards and snakes are ovoviviparous, that is, the female retains the eggs in her body where they hatch, and the young are born alive. Some species of lizards and snakes are truly viviparous — a primitive placenta actually develops.

Other major reptilian adaptations for living on land include skin which is protected by scales to cut down on water loss, and well-developed lungs, which eliminate the need for respiration through the skin. Equally important is a reproductive advance passed on to the mammals — internal fertilization.

LIZARDS
Order Squamata
Suborder Lacertilia

Lizards are the most successful and adaptable of all living reptiles. Over 3,865 species exist. They not only inhabit every continent except Antarctica but also many oceanic islands as well. There are lizards that live in trees or on the ground, that burrow, that are aquatic, and even one species, the Galapagos Islands Marine Iguana, that has invaded the sea. Lizards, while especially numerous in tropical rainforests and scorching deserts, are also plentiful in many temperate regions. A few species even range to within the Arctic Circle.

While lizards may vary in size from tiny $1^5/_{16}$ in. (34 mm) geckos to the $9^1/_2$ ft. (2.9 m) Komodo Dragon, the vast majority of these reptiles are between 5 in. (12.7 cm) and $2^1/_2$ ft. (76 cm) in total length.

Lizards are dry-skinned, scale-covered reptiles that typically have well-developed eyes with eyelids, external ear openings, four legs, five toes on each foot and a long, easily broken tail. While most lizards fit this description, a number do not.

Like snakes, male lizards have paired copulatory organs, the hemipenes. Some species are sexually dimorphic. In these taxa, males may be larger or more brilliantly colored than females. In many species, there are well-developed courtship displays by the males towards females as well as specific male to male interaction which determines which male will have the privilege of mating with a receptive female.

More than 75% of all lizards are insectivorous and play a key role in controlling the numbers of insect populations considered noxious by humans. Most lizards can be thought of as highly beneficial to home gardens and agriculture.

Five families of lizards are represented in Hawai'i: the iguanids (one species), the anoles (three species), the true chameleons (one species), the geckos (eight species), and the skinks (five species). All but four of the geckos and three, or possibly four, of the skinks have entered Hawai'i during the past 125 years.

IGUANID LIZARDS
Family Iguanidae

For most of the 20th century, the majority of lizards native to the Americas were classified as members of this family. However, in 1989, the family Iguanidae was divided into nine separate but closely related families by taxonomists. Today, the Iguanidae presently represents only about 25 species in eight genera of mid- to large-sized, diurnal, primarily New World lizards. These include Green Iguanas, spiny-tailed iguanas, chuckwallas, the Desert Iguana, Galapagos Islands Land and Marine Iguanas, and two or more species endemic to the South Pacific islands of Fiji and Tonga. All iguanid lizards feed

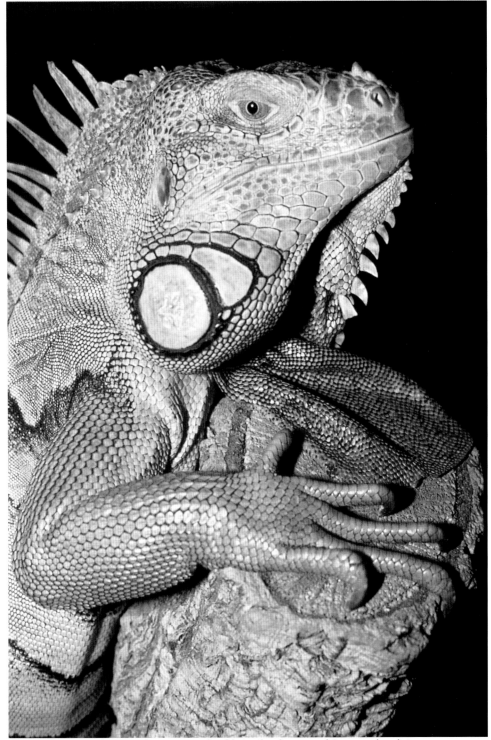

Green Iguana, *Iguana iguana*, male. Note the large subtympanic plate.

on a variety of edible plants, although most species are omnivorous. All are egg-laying (oviparous). One introduced species, the Green Iguana, occurs in the Hawaiian Islands.

Green Iguana
(Iguana iguana)

Subadult Green Iguana, *Iguana iguana.*

The Green Iguana is a large, thick-bodied 3–6$^{1}/_{2}$ ft. (1–2 m) lizard with well-developed limbs and a long, tapering tail. Despite its large size and initially

awesome appearance, it is shy and retiring and poses no danger to people, pets, or Hawaiian agriculture. This lizard occurs in low densities. It is primarily a vegetarian and feeds on brightly-colored flowers, leaves and fruit of a variety of trees, bushes, shrubs and weeds. In addition, juveniles may also include some

Juvenile Green Iguana.

insects in their diet. These lizards live in forested areas and in stream valleys on Oʻahu.

Close-up of head of a female Green Iguana.

The Green Iguana has excellent eyesight, is fast, a good climber, and very difficult to catch. If it senses danger, it will remain motionless so as to blend in with surrounding vegetation. If a potential predator moves closer, it will quickly climb up into the nearest large tree. This lizard may sometimes be encountered basking on a tree limb near water and is a good swimmer. If threatened, it will dive into the water, and with its legs against its sides and using its tail as a paddle, swim underwater to the protective cover of shoreline vegetation.

Reproduction: A male Green Iguana can be distinguished from a female by its broad head, large jowls, larger-sized throat fan and row of glandular pores on the undersurface of the hind legs. A male will display to other males to confirm territory and show dominance during courtship. Head bobbing plays a major role in social interactions. A male will distend his dewlap (throat fan)

Juvenile Green Iguana feeding on hibiscus.

and repeatedly nod his head up and down. Less dominant males will usually seek unoccupied areas nearby. Only occasionally will a fight between males ensue. Although they may receive a few scars, males typically are not seriously injured in fights over territory. As is the case with most other animals, fights between males are more ritualistic than damage-directed. Mating usually takes place 3–7 weeks before nesting. A female will select a nesting site to dig her burrow in an area that is sunlit and will lay 14–76 parchment-shelled eggs in a nest hole excavated in earth. (The author is aware of Hawaiian clutch sizes that varied between 20–63.) A reproductively active female typically lays once a year. The eggs usually incubate at temperatures between 82–90°F(28–32°C) and take 10–14 weeks to hatch. Within several days of hatching, the eggs indent slightly. This makes it easier for the hatchling to slit the flexible eggshell with one of its front claws. (This species does not have an egg tooth.) The neonates all emerge at approximately the same time. The hatchlings dig out of the egg chamber without parental assistance. Juveniles are less than one ft. (30.5 cm) in length at hatching. Males can become reproductively active as early as 15 months; females at two years. The growth rate of Hawaiian specimens is variable; those from moist valleys grow faster; those living in drier areas grow slower and typically mature at 20–32 months of age.

Identification: Juvenile Green Iguanas are bright green whereas adults are dull green, rusty brown or grayish in color. Adults frequently have some brown or gray banding. A single row of impressive spines extends along the crest of the back. A large circular shield known as the subtympanic plate is present under the ear. The dewlap (throat fan) is well-developed. The large size of this lizard immediately distinguishes adults from other lizard species in Hawai'i. Hatchlings and small juveniles may be easily differentiated from Knight Anoles by their shorter, more rounded heads and light green dewlaps. This species used to be one of Hollywood's "B" movie favorites for depicting dinosaurs and other prehistoric reptiles.

Distribution: First recorded in Hawai'i in the 1950s, reproducing iguana populations, probably descendents of escaped pets, have existed on O'ahu since the late 1950s or early 1960s. This lizard is found in disjunct populations on both leeward and windward O'ahu. It is most common in Manoa, Nu'uanu and Waimanalo Valleys. The widespread, relatively unchecked suburban development on O'ahu has destroyed some key habitat and fragmented or extirpated a number of populations of this lizard on the island. Viable populations no longer remain in 'Aina Haina, Kailua Heights, or Diamond Head. Individual wild specimens have occasionally been captured on the islands of Kaua'i, Maui, and the Big Island. However, there is no evidence of breeding populations on these neighboring islands at this time. This species is indigenous to Mexico, Central and South America. Green Iguanas became established in the state of Florida during the 1970s. In Latin America, its eggs and flesh are regularly eaten, and it is sometimes called "gallina de palo" (chicken of the tree). Since the mid 1980s, Green Iguanas have been ranched in large numbers in Central America. Several hundred thousand of these ranched hatchlings and juveniles are imported into the U.S. mainland each year for sale as pets.

Interesting Fact: During the 40+ years that Green Iguanas have been present on Oʻahu, they have never caused any recorded damage to Hawaiian plants or agriculture. This naturally low-density species is not aggressive, despite its large size. Hikers and others interested in and appreciative of wildlife are fortunate indeed if they have the opportunity to observe one in the wild. Green Iguanas are certainly deserving of "kamaaina" status.

Care in Captivity: In year-round warm climates like the Hawaiian Islands, Green Iguanas are best maintained outdoors in large, planted, screened or wire aviaries in pairs or small groups with no more than one male to an enclosure. Thick climbing branches and a large water bowl should be included. In captivity, these lizards should be offered leafy vegetables and chopped fruit in a shallow feeding pan on an every-other-day basis. Juveniles are especially fond of edible blossoms such as hibiscus. A vitamin-mineral powder should be lightly sprinkled onto the food.

Readers should be aware that wild adults generally do not make suitable pets. If forcibly captured, they will not hesitate to try to escape by biting, lashing their powerful tails and using their sharp claws. Long leather gloves should be worn when handling adults that are either wild or which have not had their claws trimmed.

At the time of publication, it was still illegal for Hawaiian residents to keep Green Iguanas in captivity. Any change in regulations must be issued through the Hawaiʻi State Department of Agriculture. Before attempting to catch or keep a Green Iguana in Hawaiʻi, be certain it is legal to do so.

ANOLES
Family Polychridae

Recently, the large family Iguanidae was split by taxonomists into nine separate, closely related families. One of these, the Polychridae, includes all anoles (genus *Anolis*) as well as several other closely related genera of lizards. All are native to North, Central and South America, as well as the islands of the Caribbean.

Anoles, genus *Anolis,* are represented by about 250 species. They are small to moderate-sized, primarily diurnal lizards, especially common in tropical regions of the Americas. Depending on the species, they vary from under 1 in. (25 mm) to over $7^1/_2$ in. (191 mm) in snout-vent length (SVL) and reach a total length of between 2 and $19^3/_8$ in. (51–492 mm). Males have well-developed throat fans (dewlaps). Each species has its own unique dewlap-extension and head-bobbing display. Most are arboreal or semi-arboreal, and all are egg layers (oviparous). Three introduced species occur in the Hawaiian Islands.

Green Anole
(Anolis carolinensis)

Green Anole, female.

Green Anole lizards were first observed in the Kaimuki district of Honolulu on the island of Oʻahu in 1950. This initial population is thought to have its origin from the release of imports available in Island pet shops at that time.

Sometimes incorrectly called the "American Chameleon," this reptile is not related to the true chameleons. However, like a number of diurnal lizards, it can vary its color between green, brown, tan, and gray. These variations are the result of rearrangement of pigment cells in the skin and are in response to such stimuli as visual contact with other Green Anoles, particular emotional state, degree of activity, as well as temperature and humidity. Males of this species attain a larger size than females.

Green Anole, male, with dewlap partially extended, after driving a non-resident male out of its territory.

This lizard has elongated toe pads with numerous transverse ridges on the undersurface, as well as claws at the tip of each toe. These aid in climbing trees, bushes, and other rough horizontal or vertical surfaces. Its long, slender tail has break points which will allow the tail to break off if it is seized by a predator. The Green Anole becomes active as soon as it is warmed by the sun's rays. Any morning dew or raindrops are lapped off surrounding foliage. This lizard typically moves at a slow pace along the tops of fences or tree limbs in search of insects and spiders to feed on. It has a strong sense of territoriality.

In Hawai'i, the Green Anole filled a new niche created by human landscape transformation. It was the first arboreal, **diurnal** insect-eating lizard. It coexists with humans and is most common in backyards, gardens, on fences, railings and on spacious hotel grounds because of the large number of introduced plants which provide suitable habitat and because of the accompanying introduced insects that also live in these areas. It is often present in lesser numbers in fields and areas of disturbed secondary growth.

Identification: The Green Anole has a snout-vent length of 2–3 in. (5.1–7.6 cm) and a total length of 5–9 in. (12.5–23 cm). Its pointed snout and relatively thin, small body easily distinguish it from the Green Iguana. Its overall smaller size and lack of a light-colored bar on the shoulder separate it from the Knight Anole. Its ability to turn green as well as its pink dewlap differentiates it from the Brown Anole, which is never green and has an orange dewlap.

Distribution: This reptile occurs throughout O'ahu, Maui, the Big Island (Hawai'i), and at some localities on Kaua'i and Moloka'i. An unrelated population of this species was introduced from Florida by a serviceman onto the Leeward island of Midway, where it is now established. The Green Anole in Hawai'i was initially misidentified in 1950 as *Anolis porcatus,* a native of Cuba. However, all Green Anoles in the Islands are actually the common southeastern United States form *Anolis carolinensis.*

Interesting Fact: Like most other lizards, the Green Anole possesses excellent color vision and is highly territorial. If a resident male encounters another male Green Anole in his territory, the resident male will turn bright green and extend his pink throat fan while laterally compressing his body and making a series of specific bobbing motions. If the intruding male does not respond through either a submissive display, which consists of a series of rapid head bobs and changing color from green to brown, or by leaving the immediate area, the resident male will approach and a fight will ensue. During this ritualized combat, the small nuchal crest (crest along the ridge of the neck) becomes erect and a dark spot appears on the skin behind the lizard's eyes. The males often lock jaws which may cause minor lacerations to the head of one or both lizards. Although these wounds may bleed lightly, they are not serious and will quickly heal. The territorial challenge usually ends when one of the males displaces the other from the branch or other elevated location on which they are fighting.

Care in Captivity: Green Anoles generally do well in captivity at home or in the classroom. A pair, or several females, can be housed in a ten gal. (38 liter) terrarium. Use topsoil for substrate. Put in two or three live potted plants as well as several medium-sized branches, placed horizontally, that extend the length of the tank. Mist the plants and anoles daily with a water spray bottle.

Female Green Anole, *Anolis carolinensis*.

Anoles prefer to lap up water rather than to take it from a water bowl. Live insects need to be offered every other day.

In Hawai'i, generally only mealworms are available as a food source commercially. However, by putting a small piece of fish or meat out in the backyard, large numbers of flies can be attracted to the bait. Using a butterfly net and by bringing it down over the bait, these can be easily captured. The contents of the net can be inverted into a clear plastic bag. This can be tied off and placed in the refrigerator for 20 or 30 seconds or just until the flies become immobile. Then the flies can be poured out onto a section of newspaper. The wing on one side of the body can be clipped off with a small pair of scissors. The flies need to be returned to the plastic bag to be dusted with a pinch of powdered vitamin-mineral supplement. Such supplements are available at most pet shops. At this point, the live flies can be emptied into the lizard's enclosure. Most small insect-eating lizards, including Green Anoles, need to be offered food on an every-other-day basis. Typically, an adult Green Anole might eat five to ten flies at a feeding.

On the U.S. mainland, two to three week-old (about one-third grown) crickets can be purchased commercially for food at many large pet shops, as can vitamin-mineral and calcium supplements with which to dust the live insect food.

Brown Anole
(Anolis sagrei)

Brown Anole, male, with nuchal and vertebral crest raised.

This small, stout-bodied, diurnal lizard was first brought to the attention of the author in Hawai'i in 1980. The Brown Anole is found in much higher densities than the Green Anole. It is less arboreal than the Green Anole, living on the ground, under or in yard shrubbery, in planters, along walkways, lumber or rock piles, or on fences and trees. It can climb, but it is unusual to see it more than 6 ft. (2 m) off the ground. When in trees, it often faces head-down and males may display in this position. If attacked or cornered, it often drops to the ground and attempts to escape by making a series of short, erratic hopping movements. This species is most common in yards, shopping malls, canal banks or other areas modified by man. It feeds on invertebrates, especially crawling forms, including ants, cockroaches, small beetles, spiders, and sometimes also on small lizards. Prey is captured by swift dashes.

Brown Anole, *Anolis sagrei*, male displaying.

Identification: The Brown Anole has a snout-vent length of $1\frac{1}{2}$–$2\frac{1}{2}$ in. (38– 64 mm) and a total length of 5–$8\frac{3}{4}$ in. (13–21.3 cm). Males are more robust and significantly larger than females. Females typically have a light, middorsal stripe, often with blotching present. Juveniles frequently have a middorsal stripe as well. Overall coloration and pattern varies, from tan to very dark brown, brownish-gray to charcoal. The neck (nuchal) crest is well-developed in males. Males also have a small body (vertebral) crest and a tail (caudal) crest. Smaller size and the lack of a pale shoulder stripe easily distinguishes this species from the Knight Anole.

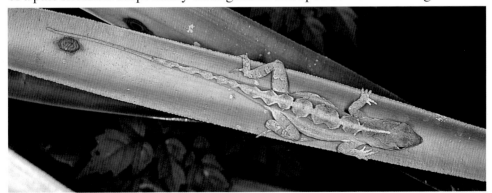

Brown Anole, female, in sleep position on a leaf.

A shorter snout, orange-red throat fan with a white or light yellow border, and the lack of ability to turn green readily differentiates it from the Green Anole.

Distribution: This species was first observed by the author in a half block area of a residential neighborhood in Lanikai on windward Oʻahu. Its range is expanding rapidly and now includes major portions of Lanikai, parts of Kailua and Kaneʻohe as well as Waikiki on the leeward side of the island. The origin of these lizards is unknown. It is speculated that they were initially released pets. This species is sold very inexpensively through the pet trade in Florida. Several subspecies of Brown Anoles are now well established in parts of Florida, with interbreeding occurring among them. Hawaiian animals are of Florida origin. This lizard has also become established in several locations in southern Mexico and Central America. It is native to Cuba, Jamaica and the Bahamas.

Reproduction: Like other anoles, this species is strongly territorial. Males head bob, do pushups, raise their crests and display their bright, well-developed throat fans to other males. If this fails to discourage the intruder, the resident male will charge his opponent. If the male still does not leave, a fight will ensue. As with other anoles, the resident male wins the overwhelming majority of battles. Mating occurs throughout most of the year. The female only lays a single egg at a time under slightly moist earth, leaf litter or surface objects. The egg can hatch in as short as 30 days. Neonates average $^{11}/_{16}$ in. (18 mm) SVL and $1^7/_8$ (49 mm) TL.

Interesting Facts: Perhaps the most striking feature of any male anole, including the Brown Anole, is its well-developed throat fan (dewlap). This flap of skin below the chin can be swung forward and downward when the lizard displays. This movement is possible because of a flexible rod of cartilage, present near the middle of the throat. When the throat fan flares out, the individual chin scales become separated and the bright display color of the fan flashes into view. The dewlap in females is small or rudimentary.

Care in Captivity: Manage in a manner similar to the Green Anole except that the enclosure should include several flat rocks and more mid-sized horizontal branches for the lizards to climb on. Hawaiian residents must check with the Hawaiʻi State Dept. of Agriculture as to whether this species can be kept in captivity.

Author's note: Brown Anoles are more aggressive than Green Anoles and develop much higher population densities. Each of these two species utilizes partially different, but overlapping ecological niches. It will be important to follow whether pressure from the Brown Anole contributes to reduced numbers of Green Anoles in Hawaiʻi. Some experts believe that the introduction of Brown Anoles in Florida is partially responsible for reduced populations of Green Anoles in that state. This species should not be released into areas in the Islands where it is not yet present.

Knight Anole
(Anolis equestris equestris)

Knight Anole.

These diurnal lizards are entirely arboreal, living in large shade trees, coconut palms and, occasionally, on fences. Specimens sometimes position themselves facing head-down on tree trunks. They rarely descend to the ground, except to occasionally take prey or for a female to lay eggs. These lizards feed on a wide variety of mid-sized and large insects, spiders, and small lizards. Large individuals are capable of taking small rodents, frogs and occasionally also consume fruits and berries.

If threatened by a predator, the Knight Anole may flee or it may stand its ground trying to appear larger and more formidable by presenting itself broadside to the threat, with mouth open and crest and dewlap extended. Knight Anoles are not as quick and agile as most other anoles. While they are not aggressive towards humans, their strong jaws and sharp teeth are capable of giving a painful bite if grabbed or handled carelessly.

Reproduction: Knight Anoles maintain large territories and are a low-density species. Males will extend their dewlap and will bob and display to each other until one retreats. Fighting between males over territory can occur but with less frequency than seen in Green Anoles and Brown Anoles. Mating occurs most often in the spring and summer. Females of this species lay one to two eggs under loose leaf litter. The eggs take 46–85 days to hatch, depending on incubation temperature. Hatchlings are dull olive brown with white spotting on the upper body and white barring on the tail.

Identification: The Knight Anole is one of the largest of any of the anoles. Adults attain a snout-vent length of 5–7 in. (12.7–17.8 cm) and a total length

Knight Anole, hatchling.

Knight Anole, female.

of between 13 and 19³/₈ in. (33 and 49.2 cm). This large, impressive lizard is easily distinguished by its wedge-shaped head and two off-white or yellowish stripes or bars. One of these stripes extends from under the eye to just past the ear opening, while the other is at the shoulder. The male's throat fan, when extended, is light pink and without spotting. It is huge, continuing from under the chin to well back on the chest. The overall color of the lizard is usually green, brown or charcoal. A small neck crest is present in males which can be elevated when displaying. Its large size readily distinguishes this lizard from other anoles in Hawai'i.

Knight Anole, *Anolis equestris*, male with throat fan extended.

Distribution: Breeding colonies of the Knight Anole have only been documented to date in Kaneohe and Lanikai, on the windward side of the island of Oʻahu. The presence of this lizard on Oʻahu was first brought to the attention of the author in 1981. The source of entry into Hawaiʻi for this species is uncertain, but they may have descended from escaped pets. Knight Anoles are established in Dade and Broward counties in Florida where they have been present since the early 1960s. They are native to the island of Cuba. All Knight Anoles in the pet trade are wild-caught Florida specimens so Hawaiian specimens are of Florida origin.

Care in Captivity: Because of their large size, Knight Anoles need to be housed in large enclosures with thick branches for climbing and, if indoors, an overhead light must be present for them to bask under. They feed on large insects and newborn (pinkie) mice, and need to be fed every other day. Members of this species must be handled carefully as they are capable of giving a painful bite. In captivity, Knight Anoles are more suited as a display animal than one which is frequently handled.

At the time of publication, it was illegal to keep Knight Anoles as pets in the state of Hawaiʻi. Hawaiian residents wishing to keep this species in captivity must first check with the Hawaiʻi State Department of Agriculture to determine if it is legal to do so.

54

CHAMELEONS
Family Chamaeleonidae

There are over 130 described species of Old World chameleons. Most are native to Africa or to the large island of Madagascar. As a group, they are highly specialized, arboreal, insectivorous lizards. Chameleons are particularly fascinating because of three adaptations: their ability to change colors, hues, and patterns quickly; the fact that their eyes, set on turrets, move independently of each other; and the remarkable tongue, which can be shot out of the mouth with considerable speed to capture prey at a distance greater than the length of the lizard's body. The word "chameleon" has become synonymous with color change.

As a result of recent phylogenetic analysis, taxonomists have reclassified chameleons. They are now considered to be related to the agamid and iguanid lizards and have been placed in their own subfamily within the Chamaeleonidae.

Jackson's Chameleon
(Chamaeleo jacksonii xantholophus)

Jackson's Chameleon capturing insect prey.

This lizard is highly specialized for living in bushes and trees. It has opposable toes on all four feet for sure footing, even on slender branches. It can flatten its body from side to side to resemble a leaf, or make its body thinner and more elongate to resemble a tree branch. In addition, independently swiveling eyes set on turrets not only provide the lizard with both independent and

Jackson's Chameleon, young adult male. Note length of the horns.

binocular vision, but also allow it to see in any direction. Recent research has shown that the chameleon eye lenses cause light to diverge which allows the eye to focus to a much finer degree than any other vertebrate animal. Often one of these reptiles will sway from side to side while approaching an insect in order to view it from several angles and gauge the distance between itself and its intended prey. The prehensile tail, which is normally coiled, can be used as a fifth grasping appendage when the lizard is moving into position to capture a prospective meal.

Chameleons are the "sharpshooters" of the lizard world. The hollow tongue, enlarged and like a moist suction cup at the tip, may be shot out by muscular contractions over a full body's length at an insect and, through the use of a second set of muscles, be withdrawn almost instantaneously. It is the movement or motion of an insect which initially attracts the lizard's attention to it. In Hawaiʻi, the versatile, but low-density Jackson's Chameleon feeds on a wide variety of primarily introduced species of insects and other invertebrates including, but not limited to grasshoppers, crickets, flies, bees, butterflies, moths, beetles, cockroaches and spiders. During hundreds of hours of field observations of this species in Hawaii, the author has seen nothing to indicate it will negatively impact endemic species of invertebrates.

Jackson's Chameleon, neonate (newborn).

Jackson's Chameleon, juvenile.

Like other Old World chameleons, Jackson's are renowned for their ability to rapidly change color. Their color repertoire includes shades of green, yellow, blue, brown, gray, charcoal, and black. These changes of color are possible through movement of pigment in the skin cells known as chromatophores. The spectacular color changes do not occur as a result of the coloration of surrounding vegetation. Rather, they are in response to the chameleon's emotional state due to such things as interaction with other chameleons of the same species, degree of activity, response to predators, intensity of light, or the temperature. These changes do serve, however, both to camouflage the chameleon and to visually cue others of its species as to its mood.

Identification: This thick-bodied lizard has an average snout-vent length (not including horns) of $4^3/_4$–5 in. (12.1–12.7 cm) and an average total length of 10 in. (25.4 cm). However, an extremely large adult male may slightly exceed 6 in. (15 cm) in SVL and be more than 12 in. (30 cm) in total length. Newborns have a total length of $1^1/_2$–$1^3/_4$ in. (38–44 mm) and weigh about 0.02 oz. (0.5 g). This reptile's specialized arboreal adaptations quickly distinguish it from other lizards in the Hawaiian Islands.

Distribution: The Jackson's Chameleon is now well established in Hawai'i. While it is most common on O'ahu in areas of mid-elevation in the Ko'olau Range between Kane'ohe and Kailua, it has a wide, disjunct distribution throughout O'ahu and can even be found at low elevations on the much drier leeward side of the island. Additionally, it is now also well-established at mid-elevation in several areas on the Kona side of the Big Island of Hawai'i and on the island of Maui. In upcountry Maui around Makawao, these lizards are most frequently encountered in secondary disturbed forest areas, in various types of orchards and on hedges in yards. The first reports of this species on the islands of Kaua'i and Lana'i were in 1995. The Yellow-crested Jackson's Chameleon is native to the slopes of Mt. Kenya in the country of Kenya in East Africa where it occurs at 6000–8000 ft. (1830–2440 m) elevation. It is the largest of the three Jackson's Chameleon subspecies.

Reproduction: Jackson's Chameleons are sexually dimorphic. The adult male has three horn-like projections at the front of the head. These include one horn over each eye and a third at the tip of the snout. Females of this subspecies typically lack horns. Males will use their horns to ritualistically spar for territory or for rights to mate with a female. After locking horns, the losing male is pushed off the tree limb and retreats. The dominant male will approach a female and signal his intent by making a series of lateral head-bobbing movements and will show yellows and blues as part of his courtship coloration. If the female is ready to mate, her solid green body color will indicate that to the male. If she is not receptive, she will show stress colors which include large areas of black mottling. Additionally, she will act aggressively by opening her mouth, hissing and attempting to bite. If the female is receptive, the male will continue his approach and mounts her from the rear. The gestation period is five to ten months. While gravid (pregnant), the female will spend more time basking and increases her food intake until the very last stages of her pregnancy when her appetite decreases markedly.

Birthing usually takes place in the morning. Each of the neonates is born encased in its own membrane. The female remains at an elevated location during the birthing process which may last from one half to eight hours. The drop from the tree branch which the female is on to the ground below stimulates each newborn to emerge from its surrounding membrane. Generally, larger,

Jackson's Chameleon, adult male.

Jackson's Chameleon, female showing threat display behavior towards a male.

older females produce larger litters. The minimum number of young recorded is five and the maximum, 50. The young disperse and are ready to feed within hours of their birth. Initially, they are rather clumsy at capturing prey. With practice, they will become efficient insect predators. The newborns and small juveniles have limited color change abilities, although the throat fan can become a maroon color at this age if the lizard is stressed. By three to four months, their color change abilities are well-developed. They reach young adulthood at seven to ten months of age.

Interesting Fact: Hawaiian Jackson's Chameleons have all descended from several dozen specimens. In 1972, a Kane'ohe pet shop owner, Robin Ventura, received a Hawai'i State Dept. of Agriculture permit to bring in Jackson's Chameleons for sale. They arrived thin and dehydrated, so he released the lizards into his backyard on Kane'ohe Bay Drive, figuring they could be retrieved later, as needed. The chameleons increased in numbers and by the late 1970s had spread to the nearby secondary growth watershed area at the base of the Ko'olau Mountains. The country of Kenya stopped exporting this species in 1981. So, virtually every Jackson's Chameleon of this subspecies in captivity on the U.S. mainland is of Hawaiian origin or has Hawaiian "roots." In the Islands, this lizard is one of the most popular animals with young people and is widely kept as a pet.

Care in Captivity: Jackson's Chameleons need specialized care if maintained as pets. Otherwise, they will do poorly and quickly die. They need to be housed individually. In Hawai'i, it is best to maintain these lizards in outdoor enclosures year round because they require both natural sunlight and fresh breezy air during the day as well as cool temperatures at night. These requirements can be met by building a sturdy, quarter-inch hardware wire or screened, wood-framed enclosure. Quarter-inch hardware or aviary wire is more heavy duty than screen and will also help to keep out potential predators, such as cats or rats. Where you place the enclosure is also important. It should be built around one or more flowering bushes in your backyard, or around a large potted flowering plant on your lanai. The area you select must offer opportunities for both sun and shade. If you live at low elevation where, during parts of the year, it regularly gets above 88°F (31°C), choose a location that gets morning sun but that is shielded from afternoon sun. (Exposure to excessive heat could result in the chameleon's demise.) Either a water drip system can be at-

Two male Jackson's Chameleons using their horns to spar over territory.

tached to the top of the enclosure and set to gently drip throughout the day or, at least twice a day, the enclosure should be sprayed using a garden hose or sprinkler. It is necessary for the water to drip down onto the plant leaves from which the chameleon can drink. Chameleons generally need dripping water, which simulates natural rainfall. Most will not drink from a water bowl.

Another advantage of using quarter-inch hardware wire or slightly larger aviary wire in place of standard plastic screening in Hawai'i to build the enclosure is that flies, bees and other insects will be able to enter to feed on the nectar from the flowering plants and these will be eaten by the chameleon. It is also easy to attract additional flies to the enclosure. This can be accomplished by putting in one or two flat, elevated platforms next to one of the bushes. A small piece of meat or fish, replaced daily, on this "feeding station" should supply flies for the chameleons during much of the year. Commercially raised insects are difficult to obtain in Hawai'i. A sweep net or butterfly net used in tall grasses next to a road or in areas of secondary vegetation often yield large

Jackson's Chameleon, male utilizing binocular vision.

numbers of suitable insects which can also be fed to your lizard. These need to be alive as the chameleon is attracted to specific movements that the insects or other invertebrates make. Chameleons prefer a variety of different insects in their diet. It is also important that the insects are of a suitable size. Juveniles will require smaller insects. In addition to insects, adult Jackson's Chameleons can occasionally also be offered newborn ("pinkie") mice.

On the U.S. mainland, unless you live in coastal California, you will need two enclosures, one indoor and one outdoor. If your outdoor enclosure is built around a large flowering bush, during those warmer parts of the year when

Jackson's Chameleon, female.

many insects are present, your chameleon can catch most of its own food and may only need to be supplementally fed. Observe its feeding efforts, weight and appearance when making such a decision. An outdoor, screened (non-glass) enclosure on a patio or porch can usually provide the natural sunlight chameleons need.

Commercially raised insects should be "dusted" in a clear plastic bag or plastic jar with a vitamin-mineral powder including a vitamin D_3 source at at-least one of the three or four weekly feedings. Shake the container to thoroughly spread the powder onto the insects before feeding them to the chameleon. Many such products for reptiles are available at large pet shops in your area, through herpetoculture magazine advertisements or at reptile trade shows. It is important that feeder insects are fed nutritious, balanced diets including alfalfa, whole grain cereal like uncooked oatmeal and fresh leafy vegetables so that they have a good nutritional balance before being fed to your chameleon(s). "Power feeding" is the term used when beefing up pet store-purchased crickets for a day or two before they are fed out. Commercially prepared cricket diets are also available from some petshops and dealers who advertise in herpetoculture magazines.

S. McKeown

SMALL NOCTURNAL GECKO
IDENTIFICATION KEY

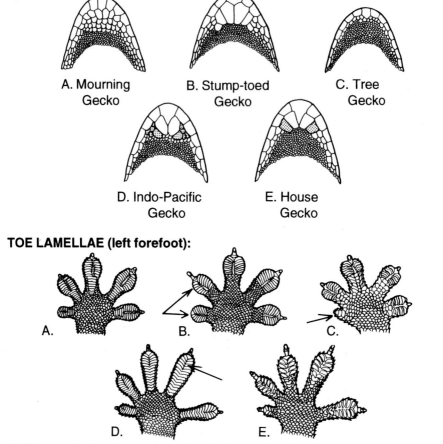

CHIN SHIELDS:

A. Mourning Gecko B. Stump-toed Gecko C. Tree Gecko

D. Indo-Pacific Gecko E. House Gecko

TOE LAMELLAE (left forefoot):

A. B. C.

D. E.

B. Note relatively wider toe pads in relation to the other species shown. C. Note rudimentary first digit. D. Note greater number of lamellae when compared with E.

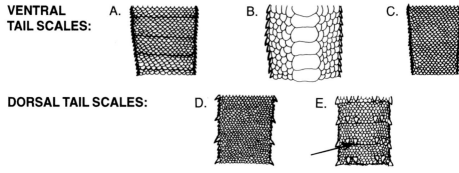

VENTRAL TAIL SCALES: A. B. C.

DORSAL TAIL SCALES: D. E.

D. Spines present at tail edge only. E. Rows of enlarged spines encircle portions of the unregenerated tail.

© *Drawings by Wesley Chun*

GECKOS
Family Gekkonidae

There are over 900 species of geckos worldwide. They are diverse, opportunistic lizards which are well-represented in warmer areas of the world. Recently, geckos were divided by several taxonomists into two closely related families, the Gekkonidae and the Eublepharidae. The eight species in the Hawaiian Islands all belong to the Family Gekkonidae. Six of these are primarily nocturnal while the two remaining species are most active during the day. Unlike most other lizards, members of this family have the ability to vocalize, making a variety of chirping, clicking or barking noises as part of their social interaction. Often these noises vary according to the situation. Specific vocalization may be for territorial recognition, courtship or to voice alarm. All eight species in the Islands have highly specialized toe pads for climbing and are arboreal. Unlike many other lizards, members of Family Gekkonidae have immovable eyelids; their eyes, like those of snakes, are always open. A gecko keeps the fixed plate covering its eyes clean by licking each eye as needed with its long tongue. All Hawaiian species are arboreal and have enlarged toe pads. The undersurface of each digit contains brush-like pads or lamellae which house many thousands of tiny, hook-like bristles or setae. Each bristle contains large numbers of suction cups which are so small that they can only be observed through the use of an electron microscope. These toe pads can fit into irregularities in almost any surface. This enables arboreal geckos to move freely on vertical planes such as walls, ceilings and even glass. On rough surfaces, such as tree trunks, the claws at the end of each toe assist in the climbing process. Most geckos, including all Hawaiian species, employ tail loss as an escape mechanism against predators. Females of many arboreal geckos store calcium in endolymphatic (chalk) sacs. These are observable on the side of the gecko's neck and are important in egg development.

Many gecko species are well adapted to living in close association with humans. They are beneficial, consuming large quantities of cockroaches, termites, mosquitos, flies, ants, moths and other noxious insects. Many geckos earn their keep in Hawai'i, in people's homes, feeding on these unwanted invertebrates.

Mourning Gecko
(Lepidodactylus lugubris)

Mourning Gecko, *Lepidodactylus lugubris.*

The Mourning Gecko may have arrived as a stowaway aboard the early Polynesian voyaging canoes or may have rafted across open ocean independently in storm debris as its eggs have been documented as being saltwater–tolerant.

This lizard has enlarged toe pads and is arboreal like other Hawaiian geckos. It usually stays hidden under bark or rocks during the day although it is sometimes encountered out, but near cover, as on the exposed root systems of large trees such as banyans and figs. When resting, the tail may be partially coiled to one side. This reptile may sometimes venture short distances from its hiding place to lick nectar or juice off ripe mangoes and papayas that have fallen to the ground. Mourning Geckos often live in houses. Some become so accustomed to those humans who enjoy or tolerate their presence, that they will crawl down to lap fruit juice off cutting boards. This lizard is gregarious, especially when not active, and a number of individuals may be found in close proximity to each other. At

Typical Mourning Gecko egg-laying site under loose bark on tree root.

night this reptile becomes active. It can be observed in and around houses and other buildings near lighted areas to which many small insects, its principal food, are attracted. This species is equally at home in residential neighborhoods or uninhabited areas.

Like other Hawaiian geckos, it has a well-developed voice, and it makes a loud single-syllable chirping noise which is repeated five to ten times in quick succession and sounds something like *"chik, chik, chik, chik, chik, chik, chik..."*

The Mourning Gecko is often cream-colored, but it can change shades of color between white, brown, reddish-brown, fawn and gray. The ventral surface is white or light yellow. Thus, it camouflages well against most wood and rock backgrounds.

Identification: The skin is smooth and satiny to the touch. A dark bar extends from the tip of the snout, through the eye, and onto the neck. Paired dark spots or inverted V-shaped barring are usually present on the back, and extend onto the tail, if the latter is unregenerated. The toes are moderately dilated. The first digit is reduced in size. The tail is slightly flattened, with small spinose scales along the edge which form a lateral fringe. An unregenerated tail is slightly longer than the SVL of the lizard. If regenerated, the tail may be quite bulbous. This is the second smallest Hawaiian gecko. Adults have a snout-vent length of about $1^3/_8$– $1^5/_8$ in. (35–41 mm) and grow to a total length of only $2^3/_4$–$3^3/_4$ in. (70–95 mm).

Reproduction: This particular species is parthenogenic. All Mourning Geckos are females and produce fertile eggs without copulating with a male. Each of these unisexual adults typically lays two (occasionally one) white-colored eggs. As the wet eggs leave the female's cloaca, she uses her hind feet to shape and position them. The eggs quickly dry, are hard-shelled (calcareous), somewhat oval in appearance, and adhere to the surface on which they are laid.

This species is a communal nester. Several individual females may lay their eggs in the same protected spot, such as under tree bark, in tree cavities or in the leaf axils of palms or *Pandanus.* so that a number of eggs may be present, all in different stages of development. Hatchlings are $^9/_{16}$–$^3/_4$ in. (15–19 mm) SVL and have a total length of 1–$1^3/_8$ inches (27–34 mm). Sexual maturity is reached at 8–10 months of age. Adults have a potential lifespan of five years or longer.

Distribution: After the House Gecko, the Mourning Gecko is the most common gecko on each of the main Hawaiian islands. It occurs as well on the smaller Hawaiian Islands of Ni'ihau, Lanai and Kaho'olawe. The Mourning Gecko is also found on many other islands throughout the Pacific and occurs as far south as Australia.

Interesting Fact: Mourning Geckos are the least shy and slowest moving of Hawai'i's geckos. At mid-20th century (1950), they were the most common species of gecko found in the Hawaiian Islands. The accidental introduction of the larger, more antagonistic House Gecko changed that. House Geckos go

Mourning Gecko utilizing camouflage.

after insects more aggressively and out-compete Mourning Geckos for food near building lights. House Geckos will also, occasionally, predate on juvenile Mourning Geckos. Additionally, the smaller asexual adult Mourning Geckos frequently move further from the light source "feeding stations" as an avoidance response to the more antagonistic House Geckos. Nevertheless, Mourning Geckos remained relatively abundant on Oʻahu until the 1990s. Now, however, Mourning Geckos are becoming increasingly uncommon in many localities. This is directly due to heavy predation by Red-vented Bulbuls. These illegally introduced, highly undesirable Southeast Asian birds have decimated Mourning Gecko populations. These bulbuls are also negatively impacting Hawaiʻi's other small lizards, its endemic birds, endemic invertebrates and its fruit and flower crops. Every effort must be made to keep bulbuls from becoming established on neighboring Hawaiian Islands.

Care in Captivity: Mourning Geckos do well in captivity and can be housed together in larger numbers than other Hawaiian geckos. Since they are highly social and asexual, they typically form stable dominance hierarchies. Up to four can be housed in a standard five gal. (19 liter) reptile terrarium with a sliding screen lid and up to eight in a ten gal. (38 liter) enclosure of similar design. However, when kept in groups, it is essential that each Mourning Gecko has its own separate hide area. Use several inches of earth for substrate, one or two live potted plants, as well as thick horizontal branches for climbing. Include a number of large curved pieces of bark for lizards to hide under and to use as egg-laying stations. Hollow logs can also be used for the same pur-

Mourning Gecko with replacement tail.

poses. A shallow water dish such as a plastic jar lid with large pebbles sticking out of the water (to prevent insect prey from drowning) can be placed at one end. Mist the enclosure once daily with water and moisten portions of the substrate daily as well. Mourning Geckos need an enclosure temperature of 75–85°F (24–29°C). Natural spectrum lighting is not necessary. Feed small insects every other day. Flightless (vestigial-winged) fruit flies and crickets (feed only hatchling and first stage) can be cultured as ready food sources. Also include a slice of ripe papaya or jar lid partially filled with fruit baby food. Use a powdered vitamin-mineral supplement and a powdered calcium carbonate supplement to sprinkle onto the insect food before feeding them to the lizards.

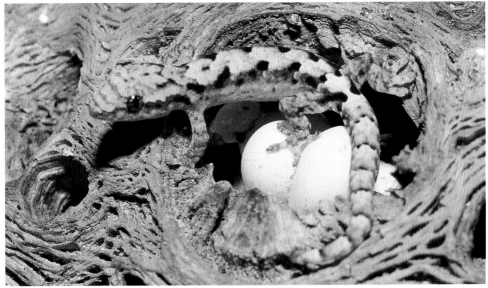

A juvenile Mourning Gecko next to communal egg deposition site.

Stump-toed Gecko
(Gehyra mutilata)

Stump-toed Gecko, *Gehyra mutilata*.

The stout-bodied Stump-toed Gecko has an uncanny ability to vary its body color to blend in with almost any brown, gray, or off-white background. If foraging for insects near a light on the side of a building at night, it is whitish and almost transparent. When on tree bark, it is usually a deep chocolate brown or charcoal-colored with small white spots.

Before the arrival of the House Gecko in the Hawaiian Islands during the mid- to late 1940s, the Stump-toed Gecko lived equally well in uninhabited areas or in close association with humans. It has largely been displaced by the House Gecko around building lights and porch lights over door entryways. It is now more often encountered around warehouses, large buildings, in lumber piles, amidst debris, under rocks, fallen palm fronds, inside rock piles and on the roots, trunk and under the bark of banyan, monkeypod, and other large shade trees. It is also commonly found in leaf axils of palms and *Pandanus*. This species is typically inactive during the day and ventures forth at night in search of food. Like other Hawaiian geckos, it is territorial.

Identification: Adults have a snout-vent length of $2^7/_8$–$2^1/_2$ in. (48–64 mm) and a total length of about $3^3/_8$–$4^1/_2$ in. (86–115 mm). Hatchlings are $^3/_4$–1 in. (18–25 mm) SVL. The head is of moderate size, slightly flattened with a rela-

Stump-toed Gecko with replacement tail.

Stump-toed Gecko utilizing camouflage.

tively short, partially rounded snout. A thin, dark stripe may be present in front of and behind the eye. Irregularly placed dark and light spots are often present on the head and body. Light barring may be present on the tail with the bars extending completely across the dorsal surface. This relatively thick-bodied species has broad toe pads and a thick ventrally flattened tail which is often constricted at the base. It is charcoal, gray or grayish-brown when inactive during the day and whitish at night when active. Ventrally it is light yellow or cream-colored. Its heavy build and wide median row of ventral tail scales readily distinguish it from the Tree Gecko, the only other Hawaiian gecko with such wide toe pads. (See Small Nocturnal Gecko Identification Key.)

Reproduction: Males have well-developed femoral and preanal pores. Males and females intertwine their bodies during mating. The male inserts one of his hemipenes into the vent (cloaca) of the female. Within several weeks, the female lays two moist, white eggs are laid in a sheltered place, such as in palm leaf axils and beneath loose bark. When they dry, the eggs are hard-shelled, almost round, and adhere to the surface on which they are laid. They take less than two months to hatch. Newly hatched juveniles are $3/4$–$7/8$ in. (19–23 mm) SVL and have a total length of about $1 9/16$–$1 15/16$ in. (40–49 mm).

Distribution: This lizard is present on all the main Hawaiian Islands as well as on the smaller islands of Lanai and Kahoʻolawe. It may have arrived as a stowaway with early Hawaiians or possibly may have rafted out to the Hawaiian Islands on debris. It also occurs in other areas of Polynesia and Micronesia.

Interesting Fact: This gecko has one very alarming escape mechanism. If seized tightly, it will twist in a person's hand causing it to slough off large pieces of its skin, exposing bare, pink flesh. This technique appears effective both against bird and mammalian predators.

Care in Captivity: House in pairs. Do not keep more than one male in an enclosure. Otherwise, manage this species in a manner similar to what is outlined for the Mourning Gecko (L. lugubris). However, although one of these lizards may be allowed to crawl onto your open hand, do not attempt to restrain it or rips to the reptile's skin may result.

Tree Gecko
(Hemiphyllodactylus typus)

Tree Gecko, *Hemiphyllodactylus typus.*

Tree Geckos are different from other small nocturnal Hawaiian geckos in two respects. They do not typically live in association with humans, and they are not generally gregarious, at least when active. Instead, they live in forested areas and stream valleys and may be found under tree bark, in leaf axils of palms, in rock or lumber piles, or amidst debris. Rarely, they may be encountered on the sides of buildings at night or inside homes in rural areas, but generally further from the light bulb or other light source than nocturnal geckos of other species. They are the least commonly seen small nocturnal gecko in the Hawaiian Islands. It is likely that their numbers will continue to dwindle in the face of continuing urbanization, habitat modification and competition, as well as potential predation from House Geckos and Tokay Geckos.

These lizards feed at night on small insects. Their lidless eyes are protected by a fused transparent membrane which resembles a permanent "contact lens." The long tongue is used to lick dust, raindrops, or other particles off the eye surface. Members of this species do not vocalize as frequently as other nocturnal Hawaiian geckos.

Tree Geckos are the smallest species of Hawaiian gecko, averaging $1^1/_4$–$1^3/_4$ in. (32–45 mm) SVL and only $2^1/_4$ to $3^1/_2$ in. (58–89 mm) in total length. Hatchlings

Tree Gecko.

are $^9/_{16}$–$^{11}/_{16}$ in. (15–17 mm) SVL. The head, body, and tail are very slender. The body is covered with small granular scales. The thin tail, which is usually orange ventrally, lacks tubercles, and is rarely longer than the combined length of the lizard's head and body. This lizard may change colors between white, light gray, gray, light or dark brown or charcoal. When active at night, it is light-colored, and the body organs may be partially visible under the skin. The ventral surface is light, often with speckling.

Identification: Two thin dark stripes, one on each side of the head, extend through the eye to the shoulder. Tiny white flecking may be present at irregular intervals for the length of the dorsal surface. Two prominent, irregular dark spots edged in white, are situated at the base of the tail. Elongated dark spots may extend partially down the lateral surface of the tail with dark barring sometimes present on the dorsal surface of the tail as well. No paired dark spots or bars are present at mid-body as on the Mourning Gecko. Also, the chin shields bordering the mental plate are not enlarged as in the Stump-toed Gecko. The snout is more elongated; the head, body and tail substantially narrower; and the tail decidedly less constricted than in the Stump-toed Gecko. The toe pads are broad. However, the first digit is rudimentary and without a claw. (See Small Nocturnal Gecko Identification Key.)

Reproduction: Regardless of the size of the femoral pores, all Tree Geckos are females. Reproduction for this species is by parthenogenesis. A female normally produces two eggs which are pliable when laid, but quickly harden and adhere to any surface. Typically they are laid under bark or in some other protected location. The eggs take one to two months to hatch.

Distribution: In addition to inhabiting all the larger Hawaiian Islands as well as the smaller island of Lanai, this lizard is widely distributed on other tropical islands of the western Pacific. Its ancestors may have rafted on debris to the Hawaiian Islands or arrived with the early Polynesians.

Interesting Fact: Like other nocturnal Hawaiian geckos, this species has vertical eye pupils. During the day, the pupils contract so that only a small vertical slit shows in bright light. At night, when it becomes dark, the pupils widely expand (dilate). The elliptical pupil opening (aperture) allows for greater expansion and contraction of the pupil to occur, thus providing better night-time vision. Additionally, nocturnal gecko lizards can reduce the pupil opening to a variety of unusual shapes and patterns in response to sudden light or darkness.

Care in Captivity: House two to four lizards to a five gal. (19 liter) terrarium. Otherwise, use the care instructions outlined for the Mourning Gecko *(L. lugubris)*.

Indo-Pacific Gecko
(Hemidactylus garnotii)

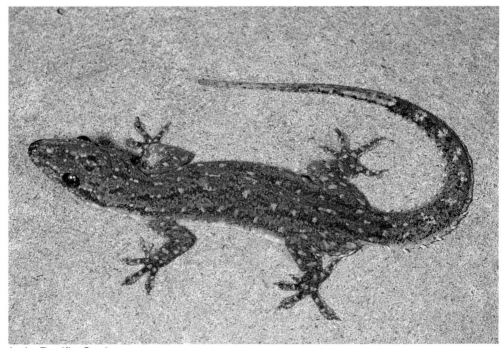

Indo-Pacific Gecko.

The Indo-Pacific Gecko is sometimes also called the Fox Gecko because of its long narrow "fox-like" snout. It is a member of a tropicopolitan genus re-

Indo-Pacific Gecko, *Hemidactylus garnotii.*

nowned for its ability to live in close association with humans. Like most of Hawai'i's other geckos, it is beneficial because of the large quantity of noxious insects and other small invertebrates it eats including small cockroaches, ants, termites, fleas, mosquitos, beetles, moths, caterpillars, silverfish, and spiders. In turn, it is preyed upon by birds including, but not limited to: bulbuls, mynahs, and short-eared owls, as well as mice, rats, large spiders and occasionally, mongooses, cats, and Giant Toads.

Indo-Pacific Geckos are most active at night, although they may rest in the open near a favorite hiding place during the day, opportunistically feeding on any insects that happen by. These geckos may be encountered most frequently under rocks at the base of trees or in rock piles during the day or on the bark of trees at night at areas of both low- and mid-elevation in the Hawaiian Islands.

Indo-Pacific Gecko, ventral view.

Indo-Pacific Gecko, hatchling.

Identification: Unlike the House Gecko, the outer pair of postmental chin shields are separated from the infralabials by one or more smaller scales. There is a *single* row of enlarged spine-like scales along the lateral edge of the tail. (These are absent on replacement tails.) The tail itself is *ventrally flattened* and generally salmon pink-colored underneath. (See Small Nocturnal Gecko Identification Key.)

Reproduction: The Indo-Pacific Gecko is parthenogenic (unisexual). The gravid female parent lays two brittle-shelled eggs in a protected spot. These hatch in one to two months. Hatchlings need about nine months to reach sexual maturity. Adults are $1^{15}/_{16}$–$2^{1}/_{4}$ in. (49–57 mm) SVL and attain a total length of $3^{3}/_{4}$–$5^{1}/_{2}$ in. (99–140 mm). Hatchlings are $^{7}/_{8}$–1 in. (23–25 mm) SVL. This lizard has the ability to change patterns and hues between white, tan, gray and charcoal and blends well with its immediate surroundings.

Distribution: Although occurring in localized areas on all the larger Hawaiian Islands as well as on the smaller islands of Niʻihau, Lanai and Kahoʻolawe, it is becoming increasingly rare. This lizard also inhabits many other islands of the western Pacific and probably arrived in Hawaiʻi with the early Polynesians in their voyaging canoes. It is widely distributed in warm climate lands bordering the Pacific and Indian Oceans.

Interesting Fact: Although still found in most Hawaiian life zones from dry coastal areas to moist, inland forested regions, this lizard has all but disappeared from urban areas, especially around porch lights, where 40 years ago it was common. This is believed to be due primarily to its inability to compete successfully in Hawaiʻi with the more aggressive, non-parthenogenic House Gecko, a post-World War II immigrant. Studies have shown that male House Geckos are better at defending and retaining their living area in territorial disputes both with female house geckos and Indo-Pacific geckos.

S. McKeown

House Gecko.

Care in Captivity: Two Indo-Pacific Geckos can be housed in a five gal. (19 liter) or three in a ten gal. (38 liter) terrarium. Otherwise, manage these lizards in a similar manner as outlined for the Mourning Gecko *(L. lugubris)*.

House Gecko
(Hemidactylus frenatus)

House Gecko, *Hemidactylus frenatus.*

The House Gecko is thought to have arrived in Hawai'i as a stowaway amidst the large amount of equipment and materials moved between Pacific islands in the 1940s, during or just after World War II. It was initially identified in Kailua on O'ahu in 1951 by Paul Breese, then director of the Honolulu Zoo.

House Geckos thrive around human dwellings. These lizards are typically found in such places as near light fixtures at night, on the sides of buildings, in houses on walls and ceilings, in cupboards, between wood slats, and behind refrigerators and other appliances. They frequent other structures including storm drains and stone walls and are common in piles of lumber, rocks or other debris. House Geckos can also be found on fences and large trees as well as in secondary-growth forests.

The bulk of their food consists of a wide variety of insects, small spiders and other invertebrates. However, adults will also consume juvenile geckos as the opportunity arises. The author has observed this species in Hawai'i feeding on

House Gecko, gravid female.

small juvenile Mourning Geckos, House Geckos and Gold Dust Day Geckos on an occasional basis.

This lizard has the ability to change shades of color between gray, off-white, and white. It is generally darker during the day while resting in a secluded place, and paler at night if near a light, so that it blends in with its surround-ings. Strongly territorial, the House Gecko is quite vocal at night. Its call is a series of quickly repeated chirps. Often it makes a squeaking noise when captured. Unlike other Hawaiian geckos, this species and the Indo-Pacific Gecko are frequently parasit-ized in the wild by tiny red mites that attach themselves between scales on the tail and the digits of the feet.

A male House Gecko may be dis-tinguished from a female by his well-developed preanal and femoral pores. A gravid female lays two round white eggs which soon dry. The eggs are

House Gecko, gravid female, ventral view.

hard-shelled and non-adhesive. Usually clutches are individual, but occasion-ally communal nest sites are utilized. This species is an opportunistic layer. Nest sites may be under loose bark, holes in trees, among palm fronds, inside human dwellings, wood piles or almost any protected, elevated location. The eggs take 45–90 days to hatch, depending on the incubation temperature. This gecko has a snout-vent length of $1^3/_4$–$2^1/_4$ in. (44–57 mm) and grows to a total length of between 4 and 5 $^1/_2$ in. (102 and 140 mm). Hatchlings average $^3/_4$–$^{13}/_{16}$ in. (19–21 mm) SVL.

Identification: Grayish-white dorsally with a peppering of tiny dark spots which may form into irregular patterns. At night when active, the color is white or pale pinkish-white. Ventrally, the color is white or pinkish-white. The digits are moderately dilated. The first digit is reduced in size with a small claw. There are rows of enlarged spiny scales that encircle the tail. The outer pair of postmental chin shields borders the infralabials. (See Small Nocturnal Gecko Identification Key.) Males can be distinguished from females by the presence of prominent femoral pores on the underside of the rear legs.

Distribution: Present on all the larger Hawaiian Islands as well as the smaller islands of Lanai and Kaho'olawe. It is also widely distributed in other sub-tropical and tropical areas of the world.

Interesting Fact: This is now the most common gecko on all the major Hawaiian Islands, not only in urban areas, but in rural and secondary forest areas as well. During the 1970s and 1980s, Mourning Geckos and Stump-toed Geckos were still the most abundant lizards near house lights at night on much of the island of Kaua'i. That has changed in most areas as the House Gecko has expanded its range and densities on that island. Now it is also the most abundant gecko species on Kaho'olawe as well.

Care in Captivity: House Geckos are best kept in pairs in a five gal. (19 liter) terrarium or in trios of one male and two females in a ten gal. (38 liter) terrarium. Manage otherwise as outlined for the Mourning Gecko *(L. lugubris)* except that slightly larger insects may also be fed to *H. frenatus*. With House Geckos, it is also a good idea to remove eggs for separate incubation as some adults may eat small juveniles.

Orange-Spotted Day Gecko
(Phelsuma guimbeaui guimbeaui)

Orange-spotted Day Gecko, *Phelsuma g. guimbeaui.*

All day geckos are in the genus *Phelsuma* which, with two exceptions, are endemic to islands in the Indian Ocean. The Orange-spotted Day Gecko is one of about sixty different taxa (species and subspecies) of day gecko. It is one of two species now established in the Hawaiian Islands. In Hawai'i, this species feeds predominantly on a variety of introduced insects and other non-native invertebrates. It will also lap pollen and nectar from flowers as well as juices from overly ripe fruit.

Identification: A thick-bodied species of day gecko with males averaging $2^1/_2$–$2^3/_4$ in. (64–70 mm) SVL, and 5–7 in. (12.7–17.8 cm) in total length. Females are $2^1/_4$–$2^3/_8$ in. SVL (57–60 mm) and 3.6–5.1 in. (9–13 cm) in total length. This diurnal lizard is one of the most attractively marked animals found anywhere in the world. When in peak activity color, it is bright green with a series of large, bright orange or orangish-red bars, lines, stripes and irregular spots present on the dorsal surface. There is a powder blue patch on the back of the head extending onto the neck. Powder blue markings may also be present on the last few millimeters of the tail. At night, or when inactive during cool weather, the dorsal color may be gray or black. Ventrally, one or two light brown, V-shaped bars and light brown spotting is present on the throat and chin. The ventral surface of the body and tail is typically a pale yellow. Juveniles are gray with white spotting. Larger juveniles and subadults can be gray with green blotching.

Distribution: In Hawai'i, this lizard is now well established in parts of Kane'ohe, Kailua and Makiki on O'ahu where it lives in suburban neighborhoods in large trees, including coconut palms and in other vegetation. First

Orange-spotted Day Gecko, male, showing comparative size.

observed on Oʻahu in the mid-1980s, the initial population is attributed to escaped pets of a hobbyist. The distribution of this lizard on Oʻahu continues to gradually expand. It has not as yet been documented from neighboring Hawaiian Islands. This lizard is native to Mauritius, an island similar in size to Oʻahu, which is located several hundred miles off the east coast of Africa, east of the large island of Madagascar.

Reproduction: Whereas most day geckos live in pairs, this species lives in small colonies consisting of a dominant male and several females. A male

Orange-spotted Day Gecko, subadult female.

Orange-spotted Day Gecko hatchling.

signals a female of his interest in mating by moving his head and neck in a series of rapid side-to-side movements. If the female is receptive, she will not attempt to flee. The male approaches and drapes part of his body over hers, sometimes grabbing the skin on her neck with his mouth. The female raises her tail and the male inserts the closest of his two hemipenes into her cloacal opening. The eggs are laid several weeks after mating in a protected spot, usually in a tree hollow or under bark. The eggs typically take between 42 and 53 days to hatch,

Eggs of Orange-spotted Day Gecko, starting to hatch.

although, depending on the incubation temperature, the incubation period may vary between 38 and 127 days.

Interesting Fact: Day geckos have often been called "living jewels of the islands of the Indian Ocean," the islands on which they naturally occur, and with good reason. Many are bright green or blue with splashes of red, orange, and yellow. These brilliant colors allow for intraspecies recognition and help day geckos camouflage themselves among the brightly-colored tropical plants and trees on which they make their homes. Orange-spotted Day Geckos are capable of rapid color change.

Protected Status: Day geckos in the Hawaiian Islands have no special protected status as of the time of publication. They are protected under Appendix II of the Convention of International Trade in Endangered Species (CITES) in their country of origin.

Care in Captivity: Since these lizards are well-established in several residential neighborhoods, some island residents simply admire the lizards living free in their yards. Hawaiian residents must check with the Hawai'i State Dept. of Agriculture to determine if this species of lizard may be kept in a confined state as a pet.

Elsewhere in the United States, the Orange-spotted Day Gecko does best in captivity if housed in large, vertically-oriented enclosures with live plants. Each enclosure may contain a single male and several adult females. This lizard prefers daytime temperatures in the mid- to high 80s°F (29–32°C), and nighttime temperatures in the high 60s to low 70s°F (19–22°C). A female typically lays two (less frequently, one) eggs. These are "glued" in place as they dry and cannot be removed without damaging them unless the eggs have been laid on a plant leaf. Therefore, it is often necessary to incubate the eggs *in situ*. This species is a colony nester. Several females may lay their eggs at the same site. Hatchlings are gray colored and vary in total length from $1^1/_8$–$1^1/_2$ in. (29–38 mm). Hatchlings should be immediately removed to their own terrarium. They are extremely shy and require a number of hiding places in their rearing enclosure. During the first week, hatchlings often refuse insects but will lick sliced papaya or a baby food/nectar mixture. This supplementation is critical for their survival. Their enclosure must also be heavily misted several times per day, as the small body size of these hatchlings permits rapid desiccation if the terrarium has too low a humidity. Up to four hatchlings of similar size may be reared together in a six to ten gal. (23 to 38 liter) enclosure. Small juveniles do best if given mid-sized branches with rough bark and are provided with live plants in their enclosures. Standard reptile glass tanks with sliding tops are not suitable for hatchlings as they are capable of fitting into the top groove and may be crushed when the top is opened. Instead, house hatchlings in a plastic terrarium with the opening at the center of the top. Place the enclosure directly under full-spectrum lighting. Proper care during the first several weeks is critical for the survival of the young. This species is uncommon in captive collections. It is very difficult to properly keep in captivity. (See the Care in Captivity section for the Gold Dust Day Gecko for additional general care instructions.) A good book on the general care and maintenance of day geckos is a must and outdoor time for the lizards in screened enclosures, weather permitting, is highly desirable.

Gold Dust Day Gecko
(Phelsuma laticauda laticauda)

Gold Dust Day Gecko, *Phelsuma l. laticauda.*

A spectacularly colored, diurnal lizard that lives in plants, bushes and trees in yards and gardens and on both the outside and inside of human dwellings. It feeds principally on introduced species of insects and other arthropods, and will also lap nectar from overly ripe fruit, and pollen from flowers.

Identification: Adults have a SVL of $2^1/_4$–$2^3/_4$ in. (57–70 mm) and reach a total length of 4–$5^1/_2$ in. (100–140 mm). When in peak coloration, this lizard is bright green with intense light-blue around the upper portion of each eye. A large series of tiny brilliant yellow dots extend from the back of the head over the entire neck area and onto the upper back. The mid- and lower-back has three large red "finger-like" markings which end in a random series of red spotting. Red barring is also present on the head and snout. The extensive yellow speckling on the neck distinguishes this species from the Orange-spotted Day Gecko and all other Hawaiian lizards.

Reproduction: The male approaches the female and makes a series of lateral head-wagging movements at the female. If she is receptive she will let him mount. A female in an egg-laying cycle may lay as often as every two to four weeks during the warmer part of the year. Usually two (sometimes one) eggs are laid in a plant leaf joint or other elevated, protected location. The eggs typically take 38–70 days to hatch depending on the incubation temperatures to which they are exposed. The hatchlings are about $1^5/_8$ in. (4 cm) in total length and resemble the adults in appearance. They will take six to eight months to reach young adulthood and become fully adult in size at nine to 12 months.

Distribution: This lizard is now widespread in localized areas throughout the island of O'ahu. It is also locally common on the Kona side of the Big Island. Breeding populations are present at other localities on the Big Island, including Hilo. This lizard has limited distribution on West Maui as well. This species is native to Madagascar and the Comoros, and several nearby smaller Indian Ocean islands off the coast of East Africa.

Interesting Fact: The well-established Hawaiian population traces its roots to just eight of these lizards brought in by a University of Hawai'i student in June 1974 and released near the campus in upper Manoa Valley on O'ahu. The presence of these lizards was first brought to the attention of island herpetologists in 1979, at which time they were established over an area about one-half mi.^{2} (0.8 km^2), living largely in yards and hedges. Once their presence in Hawai'i became known, a number were captured in Manoa by lizard enthusiasts and released near their homes in Diamond Head, Kahala, Aina Haina, Kailua and elsewhere throughout the island.

Protected Status: Day geckos have no special protected status in the Hawaiian Islands at the time of publication of this book. Internationally, they are protected under Appendix II of the Convention on International Trade in Endangered Species (CITES).

Status in Hawai'i: Residents of the Aloha State must check with the Hawai'i State Dept. of Agriculture to determine if it is legal to keep these lizards in a confined state as a pet. Many people in Hawai'i derive a great deal of pleasure from watching these beautifully colored little lizards living free in their yards and on their lanais as they are now widespread in some areas. Gold Dust Day Geckos routinely live on a variety of palms, birds of paradise, *Dracaena, Pandanus,* other yard shrubbery, as well as on and in human dwellings. When moving through their territories during the day, they often utilize fences, railings and rain gutters. The author has also observed individuals active at night around porch lights feeding on insects. These lizards provide excellent biological control of non-native injurious insects and other arthropods common in residential areas of Hawai'i including small crickets and cockroaches, flies, ants, moths, small beetles and spiders.

Care in Captivity Outside Hawai'i: When housed indoors, Gold Dust Day Geckos prefer daytime temperatures of 82–89°F (28–32°C) with a 10–12°F (6–7°C) temperature drop at night. In addition to full-spectrum overhead lighting, they also need a 50- or 75-watt sunspot lamp. The enclosure should have live plants as well as vertical bamboo shoots for egg-laying. As with all day geckos, good air flow is important. Provide water through misting the lizards on a daily basis. Adults feed on first-stage crickets, wax moth larvae and flies.

Gold Dust Day Gecko.

Juveniles need hatchling crickets or other tiny insects. Dust the insect food with a vitamin/mineral powder and calcium carbonate. Females, as with other species of day geckos, store excess calcium for their eggs in chalk sacs at the sides of their necks. In this species, the females are ready to breed right after egg-laying. Gold Dust Day Geckos are best housed one pair to an enclosure. The pair should not be separated. A female lays two (occasionally one) eggs in a protected spot, such as a hollow bamboo stem. As with other day geckos,

Juvenile Gold Dust Day Gecko.

immediately after laying, each egg is held with the hind feet until the outer shell hardens. The rear feet are used to place the eggs in a protected location, such as at a plant leaf joint or inside a section of bamboo. This species is not an "egg gluer" like the Orange-spotted Day Gecko, so the eggs can be gently removed to be artificially incubated in a lidded plastic container with small airholes in the top. The eggs should be placed on a dry, plastic jar or film canister lid over pre-moistened vermiculite or potting soil. This medium may need re-moistening at several-week intervals. Eggs should be incubated at 82–84°F (28–29°C) with high humidity. They will typically take 40–45 days to hatch at this temperature. The hatchlings are about $1^5/_8$ in. (4 cm) in total length. One to two young can be raised in a small, planted vivarium. If a good nutritional balance is maintained, a pair of the lizards can be put together to breed at nine to 12 months of age. This species reproduces well in captivity. Feed them small insects three times a week during most of the year, and twice a week during a standard two-month winter cool-down at 70–78°F (21–25°C). Twice weekly throughout the year, provide a fruit supplement in the form of a fresh slice of papaya or other soft fruit or a shallow container of fruit baby food mixed with a little honey. Lightly "dust" the food with a calcium powder of at least two parts calcium to one part phosphorus.

Tokay Gecko
(Gekko gecko)

Tokay Gecko, *Gekko gecko*, close-up of male.

Most of the Tokay Geckos in Hawai'i are thought to be descended from pets brought to Hawai'i in the late 1960s and early 1970s by servicemen returning from Vietnam or elsewhere in Southeast Asia. The Lanikai population, however,

Tokay Gecko, showing relative size.

probably originated from released pets obtained through the exotic pet trade. It was not until about 1980 that the Honolulu Zoo began receiving phone calls from Oʻahu residents asking either to identify these lizards or their loud vocalizations. In Hawaiʻi, Tokays utilize large trees such as banyan and fig, coconut palms, and occasionally are found in houses, especially in attics. They feed on a wide range of insects including cockroaches, other invertebrates, mice and even other lizards.

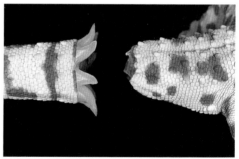

Tokay Gecko, tail loss: note break point.

Identification: This is one of the largest species of gecko lizard occurring anywhere in the world and is very distinctive in appearance. Adults of this nocturnal, arboreal species are robust and reach a snout vent length of 5–7 in. (12.7–18 cm) and a total length of 8–14 in. (10.3–36 cm). Upon hatching, juveniles average between $3^1/_2$ and 4 in. (8.9 and 10.2 cm) in total length. Males have enlarged femoral and preanal pores. Fully adult males typically have wider heads and reach a larger size than females. Males sometimes turn pale bluish-gray with extensive brick red or orange and white spotting. The background color of females tends to be more of a pale greenish-gray, usually with slightly less brightly-colored markings. Juveniles have black and white tail banding. Both sexes have numerous tubercles (raised areas) extending over the length of the dorsal surface. The ventral surface is off-white with orange-red flecking. The toes are broad with well-developed pads for climbing. The tail easily breaks off, if grabbed or pinned. That portion of the tail which is regenerated lacks tubercles.

Tokay Geckos are capable of giving a painful bite if incorrectly grabbed or carelessly handled. These lizards must either be picked up carefully or using a lightweight pair of gloves. Tokays are content to "bark" at a person who approaches their hiding place and are otherwise not aggressive. However, when it comes to being captured and there is nowhere for them to flee, they will take the offensive and bite.

Reproduction: These lizards establish territories and make a series of loud vocalizations to pronounce their ownership. The resident male will fight with other males that enter his territory. A dominant male will mate with a female. If the female remains motionless upon his approach, he will grab her by the neck with his mouth and bring his pelvic area under the female's vent before inserting one of his hemipenes. Actual mating lasts one to two minutes. A female Tokay will lay one to two (usually two) large eggs at a time. The shell is soft and pliable as the egg is being laid. The female clasps each egg alternately with her hind feet, shaping it to make it round and using her feet to place each egg in a secure location next to one another. The edge of the egg is placed against a contact surface. The eggs dry quickly in their affixed position. This species is an "egg-gluer" and the eggs cannot be removed without their being damaged. If the eggs are fertile and incubated at a warm temperature such as 79–86°F (26–30°C) with relatively high humidity, they will hatch in 2$^1/_2$–6 months depending on the specific incubation temperatures. A female Tokay in an egg-laying cycle may lay a pair of eggs as frequently as every month. The young can reach maturity in slightly less than a year.

Distribution: This species occurs in the Ko'olau mountains watershed area, above Kane'ohe and in Lanikai on O'ahu. Although fully established, its distribution is still quite limited on O'ahu. There are no reports as yet of this lizard on neighboring Hawaiian islands. These large geckos are native to Southeast Asia including the Philippines, Vietnam, Thailand, Laos, south China, Bangladesh and parts of Indonesia.

Interesting Fact: In Southeast Asia, Tokays frequently live in houses, hiding behind picture frames, furniture, or in the attic during the day and appearing on the walls and ceiling once the sun goes down. As a result of their close association with people, there are many legends and stories about these large, colorful lizards. In Asia, it is generally considered a blessing or good luck to have one or more Tokays living in your house. If a Tokay calls or makes a series of vocalizations seven times in a row, that is considered very good luck. Conversely, if a Tokay is found dead in the house or disappears, that is a bad omen for the family. Both the common names "gecko" (gek - ko) and "tokay" (tuk - koo) are derived from the sound of the calls of this large, nocturnal lizard.

Juvenile Tokay Gecko.

Care in Captivity: Hawaiian residents must check with the State Dept. of Agriculture to see if this species is allowed to be kept in captivity in the Hawaiian Islands. As of the time of publication of this book, they were not.

Mainland residents will want to keep these lizards in a vertically-oriented enclosure, the sides and back of which should be covered on the outside to give the lizards a feeling of security. During the day, these lizards need an area in which to hide, such as

Tokay Gecko hatching.

a large upside-down flower pot with a hole in one side. House singly or in pairs. **Never** keep two males together. Males are highly territorial. If they come into contact and there is nowhere for the less dominant male to flee, severe injury or death to one or both animals can occur. Feed the lizards crickets, cockroaches or newborn to 2 week-old mice two to three times a week. Include a shallow dish of either dry, crushed eggshell or shaved cuttlebone in the enclosure as an extra calcium source for females which need to replenish the calcium in their endolymphatic sacs during egg development. If a red light bulb is used, a reverse light cycle can be created if desired so that the lizards are active during the day. Include a water dish with rocks sticking out of the water so feeder insects do not drown. Also, mist each lizard daily using a spray bottle, or more often if the lizard is in the process of shedding.

SKINKS
Family Scincidae

There are over 1,300 species of skinks worldwide. They are cosmopolitan in distribution and are especially numerous in the tropics. Most are small lizards under nine in. (23 cm) in length with conical heads, smooth shiny skin, cylindrical-shaped bodies, short legs, and long, easily broken tails. Some are expert stowaways and have the ability to "raft" to islands and successfully colonize once they arrive. They are well-represented on Pacific islands where several species grow to two ft. (60 cm) in length and a number live in trees. However, the four species occurring in Hawai'i are more typical of the family as a whole. They are small, primarily diurnal, insect-eating lizards that live their lives around, on, or under leaf litter, rocks, logs, and debris.

Metallic Skink
(Lampropholis delicata)

Metallic Skink.

The Metallic Skink is a slim-bodied lizard covered with smooth shiny scales. It shares with Hawai'i's other skinks a number of adaptive modifications associated with living on the ground or under surface objects. It has a wedge-shaped head to facilitate burrowing. The external opening of the ear and the nostrils are reduced in size to keep out dirt. The flat, glossy scales offer little surface resistance. Also, the body tapers gradually which assists in propulsion and movement.

Metallic Skink, *Lampropholis delicata*.

The Metallic Skink seems to do well in areas modified by man and can regularly be found in backyards, gardens, parks and vacant lots. It is perhaps most abundant along habitat zone edges (ecotones) where secondary vegetation borders an open area such as a sunlit clearing along a field, trail, road or garden. It is just as common under large trees with elevated root systems such as banyans and figs, especially if leaf litter and/or rotting fruit or fallen blossoms are present to attract small insects, on which it feeds. This skink is uncommon or absent from thick, shaded forested areas.

This lizard is active during the day, especially in the morning. It feeds on a variety of small-sized insects including beetles, flies, mosquitos, aphids, ants, moths, crickets, cockroaches, as well as tiny worms and spiders. Prey items are crushed with its jaws and teeth and then swallowed.

Although this is now the most common species of skink in the Hawaiian Islands, it is believed to have only arrived in the Islands about 1900. The first specimen discovered in Hawai'i was in 1909 by J. F. G. Stokes in Moanalua Valley on O'ahu. At about the same time, two other lizards, the Azure-tailed Skink and the Moth Skink were documented as having become increasingly uncommon. Metallic Skinks use many of the same habitats as recorded for these latter species. How much of a role have Metallic Skinks had in outcompeting these lizards? Additional studies are needed in Hawaii to more definitively answer these questions.

Identification: This lizard has a metallic sheen to its skin and its coloration may vary slightly. The head is rust brown while the dorsal surface of the body and first third of the tail are brown or grayish-brown, often with tiny dark flecking. The remaining two-thirds of the tail is uniform gray, sometimes with a reddish-brown tinge at the tip. Striping on the sides of the body is present, but variable. The wide, uniform, dark-brown lateral stripe may be bordered top and bottom by a thin stripe, no more than one or two scales wide. The entire ventral surface is off-white or light gray. This species averages between $1^{1}/_{5}$ and $1^{7}/_{8}$ in. (38 and 47 mm) in snout-vent length and between $3^{1}/_{2}$ and 5 in. (89 and 127 mm) in total length.

Reproduction: The female Metallic Skink lays from one to seven (typically three to five) white, leathery-shelled eggs in a sheltered place, such as under leaf litter. Generally, clutch size of the eggs increases with the size and age of the female parent. Hatchlings have an average snout-vent length of $^{5}/_{8}$ in. (16 mm) and a total length of $1^{5}/_{8}$ in. (41 mm).

Distribution: A small, adaptable species, this lizard is now is found on all the larger Hawaiian Islands from sea level to areas of mid-elevation. It lives as high as 4,000 ft. (1,200 m) on the Big Island and Kaua'i. This lizard is native to Australia. Hawaiian specimens are closest in color and appearance to those from southeast Queensland.

Interesting Fact: Metallic Skinks on O'ahu are slightly smaller in size and lay fewer eggs on the average than those found on other Hawaiian Islands. One research biologist, James K. Baker, believes this may be attributable to more intraspecies competition for food and space as population densities of this lizard are highest on O'ahu, the island on which they initially became established.

Care in Captivity: As long as small insects can be regularly supplied, this species will do very well in a terrarium with soil, loose leaf litter, a few flat rocks and a small, very shallow water dish. Flightless (vestigial-winged) fruit flies and hatchling crickets can be cultured and are an ideal food source. Small insects should be provided every other day. These should be lightly dusted first in a clear plastic food storage bag with a powdered vitamin/mineral supplement. The amount of insects fed should be what is eaten in a ten-minute period after they are placed in the terrarium with the lizards.

Snake-eyed Skink
(Cryptoblepharus poecilopleurus)

The Snake-eyed Skink is the only Hawaiian skink without movable eyelids and hence the common name "snake-eyed."

Whereas the three other skinks found in Hawai'i live in a variety of habitats on the ground or under logs or debris, the Snake-eyed Skink generally prefers rock walls or areas of lava rock overlooking, or adjacent to, the beach. It is active in the littoral zone (the shore area between the high- and low-water marks). Some populations in Hawai'i, although not typically on O'ahu, do occur inland. The Snake-eyed Skink has been found at 3,200 ft. (975 m) elevation in the Kau Desert region of the Big Island. Wherever it occurs, it is often

Snake-eyed Skink, *Cryptoblepharus poecilopleurus.*

encountered sunning on rocks and, if approached, disappears into the nearest crevice. This species has relatively long legs and is quick and mobile. Because

Habitat of Snake-eyed Skink on Oʻahu.

Snake-eyed Skink.

of its alertness and agility, it is relatively adept at avoiding hungry rock crabs. An active feeder, this lizard will sometimes climb down onto the sand between the rocks and the ocean to feed on beach flies. It also eats a variety of other insects including juvenile cockroaches, tiny beetles, sand fleas, small butterflies, moths and their larvae, as well as spiders and other small arthropods.

Skinks are generally gregarious, and this species is no exception. It would be unusual to see just *one* Snake-eyed Skink living in suitable habitat. However, it is very uncommon to find Snake-eyed Skinks in association with **other** species of skinks in Hawai'i. Although primarily diurnal, this species is sometimes also active at dawn and dusk. It is a good climber and may ascend rock walls and climb trees to search for insect food. When living near large trees, leaf litter at the base of the trees is utilized for hiding. This lizard was more common in the Hawaiian Islands at the beginning of the 20th century. It is likely that development of beachfront property, resulting in loss of suitable habitat, has contributed to its decline.

Reproduction: A female Snake-eyed Skink will usually lay two (less frequently one) eggs in a protected spot. The eggs are white, oval in shape, and parchment-shelled. The eggs average $3/8$–$7/16$ in. (10–12 mm) in length. It is not uncommon for more than one female to lay her eggs in the same location. They take four to seven weeks to hatch. Hatchlings have a snout-vent length of $7/16$–$7/8$ in. (21–22 mm) and a total length of less than 2 in. (5 cm).

Identification: This lizard has immovable eyelids which cause its eyes to appear unusually large and circular, and immediately distinguishes it from any other Hawaiian skink. The dorsal color is variable, but is usually mottled brown or gray. Two thin, metallic-gold dorsolateral stripes are usually present on the head and body but these do not extend past the rear legs. The sides are black or gray with extensive white flecking. The entire ventral surface is pale yellow. This skink is $1^5/_8$ in. (43 mm) in snout-vent length and has a total length of $3^7/_8$–5 in. (98–127 mm).

Distribution: The Snake-eyed Skink has spotty distribution on all the main Hawaiian Islands, occurring on Oʻahu, Hawaiʻi, Maui, Kauaʻi and Molokaʻi as well as Lanai. It is very common in rocky areas along the coast on the small Hawaiian Islands of Niʻihau and Kahoʻolawe. This species also occurs on islands in the western Pacific and Indian Ocean.

Interesting Fact: It is not unusual to find Snake-eyed Skinks with missing toes. This may be due to attempted predation by crabs and other littoral zone crustaceans.

Care in Captivity: These lizards do well in captivity. A male and one to two females can be housed in a ten gal. (38 liter) terrarium with earth or sand as the substrate and a number of lava rocks on which to climb. Include a plastic jar lid for a shallow water bowl. Put several rocks in the water bowl so insect prey do not drown if they fall in. Feed live small insects every other day. Dust the insects in a clear plastic bag with a vitamin-mineral powder before feeding them to the lizards.

Moth Skink
(Lipinia noctua noctua)

Moth Skink, *Lipinia noctua noctua.*

S. McKeown

Moth Skink.

Juvenile Moth Skink.

The attractively marked Moth Skink is the only member of the skink family found in Hawai'i that does not lay eggs. Instead, the female typically gives birth to two live offspring, although one to four fetuses have been recorded.

This lizard, like Hawai'i's other skinks, utilizes tail loss as an escape device. If a would-be predator grabs it by the tail, that part will almost invariably snap off at one of several "breakage points." The violently writhing tail usually diverts the attention of an attacking mammal or bird predator, which allows the lizard to slip out of sight under a nearby rock or log. The skink will completely regrow a new tail in two to three months, but the regenerated caudal appendage will be shorter and less colorful than the original.

Individuals will sometimes have toes missing. This has to do with another escape mechanism. If a predator grabs a Moth Skink by a toe or limb, this lizard will rapidly twist over and over in an attempt to free itself, even if it means losing that digit.

This reptile is found in association with leaf litter both in backyards and around and on the root systems of large trees. Rock walls are another type of habitat routinely utilized by the Moth Skink in Hawai'i. If approached when on a rock wall, its escape response is to retreat into a rock crevice or crawl downward. At night, it may seek shelter under surface objects or loose topsoil.

About a century ago (1900), the Moth Skink was listed as being extremely rare in the Hawaiian Islands and was thought to have a highly limited distribution. Today, through field studies undertaken during the past 20 years by Honolulu Zoo herpetologists, we know it is much more widely distributed than previously thought. However, there are few places where it is abundant. Interestingly, the Metallic Skink utilizes many of the same habitats and microhabitats. Where encountered together, the number of Metallic Skinks typically far exceeds the number of Moth Skinks. Competition with the Metallic Skink, as well as predation by undesirable non-native mammals and birds (including mice, three species of rats, the mongoose, two species of bulbuls and cattle egrets) are the likely causes for its relatively low numbers and somewhat spotty distribution in the Hawaiian Islands today.

Identification: A prominent yellow spot is always present at the back of the head. This spot continues posteriorly as a pale middorsal stripe that fades out before reaching the tail. The dorsal color is variable, but usually light brown while the sides are generally darker. The tail is a light tan color above and off-white or gray below. As an adult, this skink has a snout-vent length of $1^1/_2$–$1^7/_8$ in. (38–48 mm) and reaches a total length of only about 3–$4^1/_4$ in. (76 mm–108 mm). Newborns are $^3/_4$–1 in. (20–25 mm) in SVL.

Distribution: It can be regularly found in Kaimuki, Makiki, Punalu'u, Laie, and many other scattered locations on O'ahu and on the Big Island (Hawai'i), Maui, Molokai and Kaua'i. This species is well represented elsewhere in Polynesia, and in Micronesia and Melanesia.

Interesting Fact: The Moth Skink is active both during the day and at dawn and dusk. Interestingly, it has also been documented in Hawai'i as remaining active well into the late evening in search of insect prey. Recent studies by herpetologist Duane Meier support these findings.

Care in Captivity: Manage in a manner similar to that outlined for the Metallic Skink *(L. delicata)*.

Copper-tailed Skink
(Emoia cyanura)

Copper-tailed Skink, *Emoia cyanura*.

The Copper-tailed Skink is a slender, active, diurnal lizard. The scales on its body and tail are small, rounded, shiny, and uniform in size while those on its head are enlarged. It has movable eyelids and, as an added feature, the lower lid contains a transparent "window" through which the lizard can see, even when its lids are closed. The longitudinal striping and different shades of color on the body and tail serve to break up its body outline and to help the lizard blend with its surroundings.

Identification: Hawaiian specimens of this lizard have three prominent whitish-colored stripes, one mid-dorsal and two dorsolateral, which extend from the front tip of the nose almost to the tail. The head is dark brown and the body lighter brown. Adults have a snout-vent length of $1^{1}/_{2}$–$1^{5}/_{8}$ in. (38–43 mm) and a total length of 4–$5^{1}/_{4}$ in. (102–133 mm). *E. cyanura* can be distinguished from its close relative *E. impar* by the following characteristics: In *E. cyanura*, the tail is copper, beige or light green color; the belly is shiny white instead of grayish-white; the paired mid-dorsal scales are never fused together to form a sequence of large single scales.

Distribution: The Copper-tailed Skink is widely distributed on South Pacific and Southwestern Pacific islands. Preliminary genetic analysis indicates

Copper-tailed Skink, *Emoia cyanura*.

the Hawai'i population is most similar to specimens from Fiji and the Cook Islands. The single known Hawaiian population, discovered in 1979 by Matt Walsh of the Honolulu Zoo reptile staff, occurs only in a small area at Po'ipu on the island of Kaua'i. Additional genetic analysis is needed to determine if these lizards represent a previously undescribed Hawaiian form or are relatively recent accidental immigrants from elsewhere in Oceania.

Reproduction: A gravid female will lay two (less commonly one) white parchment-shelled eggs under leaf litter, stones and other surface objects. Hatchlings have a snout-vent length of $^7/_8$–$^{15}/_{16}$ in. (22–23 mm).

Copper-tailed Skink, *Emoia cyanura*.

Interesting Fact: Skinks lack the ability to quickly change colors like many geckos and anoles. They do, however, share the ability to lose their tails. If grabbed or pinned, the tail easily detaches. Once severed, the tail wiggles and twitches violently. This motion will often draw the attention of the predator, allowing the lizard to make a quick exit to nearby cover. A new tail will begin to grow out within a few days. It will take several months for this growth process to be completed.

Care in Captivity: The Copper-tailed Skink in Hawai'i is far too rare to be collected or to be maintained in captivity. Unfortunately, the only known population is being decimated by a non-native bird, the Cattle Egret. The author and his associates have been in contact with the private land owner of the area which the skink inhabits as well as the State Dept. of Agriculture. Control of the cattle egrets within this small area is scheduled to occur.

Azure-tailed Skink
(Emoia impar)

Azure-tailed Skink, *Emoia impar*, in Fiji.

The Azure-tailed Skink is a slender, smooth-scaled lizard very similar in appearance to the Copper-tailed Skink. The head is slightly flattened and conical in shape. The lower eyelid is movable, with a large transparent disc surrounded by tiny opaque scales. The sleek body blends into the long tail which, if unregenerated, is $1\frac{1}{2}$ to $1\frac{3}{4}$ times the combined length of the head and body.

Azure-tailed Skink, *Emoia impar,* in the Cook Islands.

Identification: Throughout its range outside the Hawaiian Islands, most lizards of this species have a bright blue tail. However, adult and some juvenile Hawaiian specimens do not. The dorsal color is bronze to dark brown. The amount of striping in adults is also reduced. On the basis of these differences, the Hawaiian form was classified by Werner in 1901 as *Emoia schauinslandi.* However, since these differences are relatively minor, this designation is not currently recognized as valid. Adults have a snout-vent length of $1^{1}/_{2}$–$1^{7}/_{8}$ in. (40–48 mm) and a total length of $3^{7}/_{8}$–$5^{1}/_{4}$ in. (100–132 mm). Hatchlings are about $^{7}/_{8}$–$^{15}/_{16}$ in. (22–23 mm) SVL. *E. impar* can be distinguished from *E.*

Azure-tailed Skink, *Emoia impar,* in the Cook Islands.

cyanura by the presence of one or more middorsal scales which are fused, as well as a grayish-white ventral surface.

Distribution: The Azure-tailed Skink has not been sighted by scientists in the Hawaiian Islands since the mid-1950s whereas fifty years previous, at the turn of the century, it was quite common and widespread. It occurred both in dry lowland areas and in moist, wooded areas at mid-elevation. Museum voucher specimens exist for it from the islands of Hawaiʻi, Oʻahu, Maui, Kauaʻi and Molokaʻi. Outside Hawaiʻi, it is still quite common on some islands in the South Pacific and Southwest Pacific. In Fiji it is most often encountered in forested areas or along the forest edge.

Reproduction: Little data exists for the Azure-tailed Skink in Hawaiʻi. Elsewhere, on islands in the South Pacific, adults reach sexual maturity when they obtain a snout-vent length of 1½ in. (40 mm) or more. Females typically lay two (less commonly one) eggs in a protected location, such as under leaf litter or in moist soil under rocks. In Samoa, communal nesting sites have been documented with six to ten eggs to a nest. The incubation period is 40–51 days (Zug, 1991).

Interesting Fact: During the late 1800s and early 1900s, the Azure-tailed Skink was common throughout most of the Hawaiian Islands. Two factors — predation and competition — are primarily responsible for its rapid decline. The misguided intentional introduction of the mongoose *(Herpestes auropunctatus)* in 1883 from Jamaica and the accidental introduction of the Metallic Skink, have had major significance. Although the mongoose was brought to Hawaiʻi to eat rats, it has proved far more deadly to ground-nesting birds and terrestrial lizards. The Metallic Skink, which entered Hawaiʻi about 1900, is a competitor that utilizes the same types of habitat as *Emoia.* The Azure-tailed Skink is one of the most abundant lizards on many small islands in the South Pacific that have few other skink species. However, Case and Bolger (1991) have found that on South Pacific islands with a wide variety of terrestrial skinks, this species is largely absent.

Care in Captivity: If any populations of Azure-tailed Skinks are found remaining in Hawaiʻi, they should be fully protected and are, therefore, not suitable as pets. However, those with an interest in Hawaiian reptiles could provide a useful service by looking for this lizard on each of the Hawaiian Islands. Although it has not been seen since the mid-1950s, it is possible that isolated populations of Azure-tailed Skinks still exist in the Hawaiian Islands. The most likely places to look for this skink would be on Kauaʻi which, until relatively recently, was mongoose-free, and on the islands of Molokaʻi and Maui. Any skinks fitting its description that are found outside the Poʻipu area of Kauaʻi where the closely related *Emoia cyanura* occurs, can be brought to the author's attention or to the attention of Duane Meier, Supervising Herpetologist at the Honolulu Zoo.

SNAKES
Order Squamata
Suborder Serpentes

Snakes, although uniform in general body shape, are versatile in their modes of life. There are over 2,500 species. The great majority are nonvenomous and beneficial to humans. They inhabit every continent except Antarctica. Most do not "raft" well across open ocean and are thus absent from many islands, even relatively large ones such as Ireland, Greenland and New Zealand. Snakes may burrow, live on the ground, or in trees and bushes. A number live along the banks of streams and lakes. Many of the desert forms are nocturnal during the warmer parts of the year. Some species from one family are marine.

Most snakes grow to a total length of between 2 and 6 ft. (0.6 and 1.8 m) depending upon the particular species. However, snakes can vary in size from 5 in. (13 cm) blind snakes to 22 ft. (7 m) pythons. Very rarely, Reticulated Pythons, African Rock Pythons and Green Anacondas attain a greater size. The record size for the largest snake ever documented goes to a Reticulated Python which was measured at slightly over 33 ft. (10 m).

Snakes are dry-skinned, scale-covered reptiles that are very closely related to the lizards. However, snakes are distinct morphologically. Snakes lack eyelids, external ear openings, and functional limbs. All snakes are carnivorous. The quadrate bone at the back of the head and elastic muscles in the front of the lower jaw allow for maximum jaw flexibility, enabling these reptiles to swallow prey considerably larger in diameter than themselves. Most feed on rodents although some consume other mammals, birds and their eggs, reptiles, amphibians, fishes, insects and other invertebrates. Snakes swallow their food whole, without mastication. All soft parts as well as bones are completely digested. Because of the size of prey items eaten, snakes do not have to feed as frequently as most lizards, and much less frequently than the endothermic mammals.

Snakes are sensitive to surface vibrations and they can hear sound although not as well as most lizards. However, a snake's most useful sense is that of "taste-smell." When a snake flicks out its long, two-pronged tongue, it picks up chemical particles from the air. When the tongue is retracted, its tips brush against the Jacobson's organ along the inside roof of the mouth where the particles are instantly analyzed. "Taste-smell" plays a key role in the recognition of prey, enemies, or potential mates.

Possibly because of their unique elongate shape, snakes have always fascinated humans. Generally, people are conditioned to react to snakes. Those persons who have had a chance as youngsters to observe and handle snakes and are conservation/ecosystem aware, respond positively. Those persons who have not experienced these opportunities generally exhibit misunderstanding, repulsion or fear.

BLIND SNAKES
Family Typhlopidae

Blind snakes are tiny, burrowing snakes with cylindrical bodies and vestigial eyes. All species have a multichambered (tracheal) lung and the left lung is absent. Also, only the right oviduct is present. Unlike most other snakes, they have a vestigial pelvic girdle. Blind snakes feed on small insects and other invertebrates. Members of this family are widely distributed in tropical and subtropical areas of the world as well as in parts of temperate Asia and Australia. There are about 150 species of blind snakes found worldwide.

Island Blind Snake
(Ramphotyphlops braminus)

Island Blind Snake, *Ramphotyphlops braminus.*

This harmless reptile, the only species of land snake occurring wild in the Hawaiian Islands, was initially observed in 1930 on the grounds of the Kamehameha Schools, now the site of the Bishop Museum, in Honolulu. Individuals are thought to have come as stowaways in soil around the base of potted palm trees imported from the Philippines for landscaping the campus. The Island Blind Snake is completely harmless as are the great majority of snakes throughout the world. It is beneficial to humans because it eats large quantities of termites, other small, soft-bodied insects and insect larvae.

This small, secretive snake, externally almost worm-like in appearance, is well adapted to a burrowing life. It has vestigial eyes which appear as two tiny dark spots beneath the head scales, a short, rounded head, a countersunk lower jaw and a short, blunt tail with a small spine at the tip that may aid in subterra-

Island Blind Snake.

nean movement. The dark underground environment in which it lives places a premium on the senses of taste, smell and touch rather than on sight. The number of teeth are reduced. It has only a single enlarged tooth on either side of the lower jaw.

This snake must live in loose, slightly moist soil or leaf litter because the small uniform scales covering its body do not prevent drying out, and prolonged desiccation can cause death. It frequents shaded gardens and moist valleys and may be found under potted plants, plastic liners, large stones, logs and debris. During drier parts of the year, individuals burrow under root systems of bushes and small trees which retain moisture, or deeper into the soil to where the moisture levels are suitable.

Identification: The Island Blind Snake is dark gray or black above and lighter ventrally and is almost always under 8 in. (20 cm) long and very thin. However, shortly before it is ready to

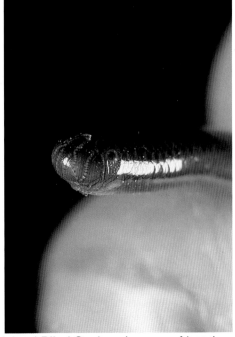

Island Blind Snake, close-up of head.

shed, the outer layer of skin loosens, causing the snake to take on a light blue appearance. It remains this color until it sheds off the old, outer layer of skin four to ten days later.

Distribution: This species has successfully colonized all the main Hawaiian Islands as well as other warm-climate areas in diverse parts of the world. It is native to Southeast Asia and the Philippines but has dramatically increased its range by dispersing with modern man in soil and in potted plant shipments.

Interesting Fact: Island Blind Snakes are parthenogenic (unisexual). All individuals are females. The eggs, white, elongate and two to seven in number, develop without fertilization by a male. Because only a single female is needed, parthenogenic species of reptiles are often successful at extending their ranges or becoming established on islands. Parthenogenesis is more common with lizards. In fact, *Ramphotyphlops braminus* is the only known species of snake that is unisexual.

Care in Captivity: One or several Island Blind Snakes can be housed in a five gal. (19 liter) terrarium. Several inches of sandy, loamy topsoil are required for the substrate. The soil should be loose and slightly moist. Mist down the top layer of soil daily. If the soil becomes too dry, dessication, resulting in death, can occur. A very shallow water dish such as a plastic jar lid should be provided at one end of the enclosure. Include one or more small live, potted plants and several flat pieces of wood to provide a surface area under which the snakes can burrow in the enclosure. A steady supply of live termites and/or ant larvae is needed for food. Approximately 20 to 25 such prey items for each snake should be provided twice weekly. After grabbing a termite, the Island Blind Snake typically breaks off the hardened jaws by brushing the head of each termite against a hard surface before swallowing the body. In Hawai'i, these snakes can be kept at room temperature. Elsewhere, a heating pad set on low or a heat tape should be placed under the enclosure to provide warmth; a 79–84°F (27–29°C) temperature range is ideal.

SEA SNAKES
Family Elapidae
Subfamily Hydrophiinae

There are approximately 55 species of sea snakes. They are distant relatives of the cobras that have adapted to life in portions of most of the world's warm oceans. Sea snakes typically have a laterally compressed body and a flat oar-like tail as well as other anatomical, physiological, and behavioral adaptations for living in a marine environment. All are live-bearing. Sea snakes are **venomous**, but are not generally aggressive towards humans. Most stay close to land along coasts, and only one, the Yellow-bellied Sea Snake, is truly an open-ocean (pelagic) snake.

Yellow-bellied Sea Snake
(Pelamis platurus)

Yellow-bellied Sea Snake, *Pelamis platurus*.   VENOMOUS

The Yellow-bellied Sea Snake, a member of the Subfamily Hydrophiinae, is both the most widely distributed and the most specialized ocean-dwelling snake. Its adaptations for living in the open ocean include a compressed body with a well-developed ventral keel and an elongated, somewhat flattened snout with dorsal valvular nostrils that close when the animal submerges. Additionally, all sea snakes have head "salt glands" which allow them to get rid of excess salts.

The Yellow-bellied Sea Snake can be found in the sea around the Hawaiian Islands. It is most commonly seen in Hawaiian waters in "El Niño" weather years. This reptile lives its entire life in the ocean. An excellent diver, it can stay submerged underwater for up to two hours before resurfacing for air. Should one of these snakes become stranded on the beach by the tide, the shape of its keeled ventral surface makes it difficult for it to return to the sea.

This marine snake is **venomous** but not aggressive towards people. No bites have been recorded in Hawaiian waters or on Hawai'i's beaches. However, the neurotoxic qualities of the venom, not unlike those produced by cobras and kraits, are highly toxic to humans and capable of causing severe muscle, kidney, and/or nerve damage, and even death. The venom is injected through one or both permanently erect hollow fangs. These are located on each side of the head inside the upper jaw below the third scale down from the tip of the snout. These fangs are connected by ducts to venom glands located at the rear of the head.

Yellow-bellied Sea Snakes typically swim at the surface as they cross open expanses of ocean. Schools of small fish mistake the snake for floating debris and swim beneath it. When it is hungry, the sea snake begins swimming back-wards. The fishes swimming under it also reverse direction to regain the as-sumed cover of the snake. This brings the small fishes close to the sea snake's head. Using a quick, specially adapted, sideways strike, the prey is easily caught. This specialized feeding technique has not been observed with other snakes. While small fishes are rapidly swallowed, larger fish are firmly gripped until movement ceases. The fish is rapidly paralyzed from the effects of the venom. Numerous large backward-curving teeth position the fish. Using its jaws, the sea snake "jaw-walks" the prey into position for swallowing.

While most land snakes shed their outer layer of skin three to five times a year, Yellow-bellied Sea Snakes shed much more often. In captivity, healthy adults have been recorded as shedding as frequently as every 14 days. Not many opportunities exist to brush against objects to assist in shedding in the open ocean. As a further adaptation to living at sea, this snake often utilizes knotting behavior, by coiling its body into tight knots and then crawling through these knots. This unique knotting behavior helps individuals to shed and also to free themselves of external marine parasites such as barnacles.

During courtship and mating, males and females intertwine their bodies as they glide through the water. This species of sea snake is live-bearing. Three to six or more young are born in the open sea. Each emerges from the female parent, tail-first, and is about ten in. (25 cm) long at birth. For several hours, the hatchlings retain their umbilical cords and attached tissues. The umbilical scar itself disappears with the first shedding. Color and pattern, including the spotting on the paddle-shaped tail, varies with each individual snake.

Identification: In Hawai'i, the Yellow-bellied Sea Snake is easily recog-nized by its valvular nostrils, a laterally flattened, ventrally keeled body, and a

Yellow-bellied Sea Snake. VENOMOUS

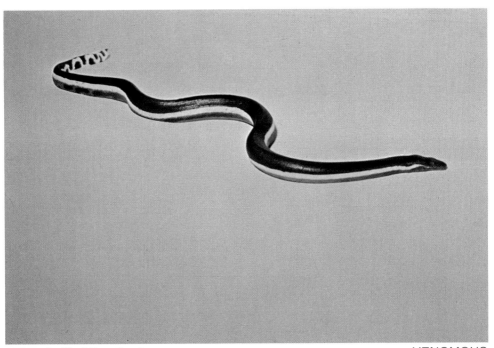

Yellow-bellied Sea Snake. VENOMOUS

paddle-shaped tail. Its dorsal surface is purplish-black. The lower sides of its body are yellow and the ventral surface is black or grayish-black. The tail is black and yellow spotted or barred. This reptile grows to between 24 and 34 in. (61 and 86 cm) in total length.

Distribution: The Yellow-bellied Sea Snake lives in warm waters of the Pacific Ocean from Central America to Australia, and the Indian Ocean. Its habit of riding the currents takes it over great distances. In Hawaiian waters, this species is encountered most often in the open ocean by fishermen spotlighting at night.

Interesting Facts: Sea snakes are shaped like eels. Both can be found in the seas around the Hawaiian Islands. Some of the smaller, more colorful eels are often mistaken for sea snakes by people snorkeling or diving. Eels, of course, are fish. They have slimy, not scaly, skin. Eels also breathe through gills, rather than lungs. In Hawaiian waters, eels can typically be found in reef areas. In contrast, the Yellow-bellied Sea Snake is much less common in shallow water and is usually encountered swimming in the open ocean.

Care in Captivity: Sea Snakes are illegal for private individuals to maintain in captivity in Hawai'i, in part because they are venomous. However, Island residents and visitors can sometimes view Yellow-bellied Sea Snakes on display at the Waikiki Aquarium in Kapiolani Park on O'ahu.

TURTLES
Order Testudines

Turtles, or chelonians, as they are also collectively called, are built for defense and look much like their ancestors did over 200 million years ago. The most characteristic feature of any turtle is its shell. The plastron (lower or ventral portion of the shell) is joined on each side by a bridge to the carapace (upper or dorsal portion of the shell). In most species, the bony shell is covered with horn-like plates. However, in a few taxa like the softshell turtles and Leatherback Sea Turtle, the shell is covered by layers of flexible skin and has a rubber-like appearance. Openings at the front and rear of the shell allow for the extension of the head, four limbs, and tail.

Turtles breathe through lungs, although some aquatic species can absorb additional oxygen from the water through the walls of the cloaca and pharynx.

Turtles lack teeth but most have jaws with sharp ridges to cut and tear food. Some are vegetarian while others are omnivorous, or even carnivorous. Chelonians are amorous creatures. Many species engage in elaborate courtship behavior prior to mating. Each male turtle has a single penis which is housed inside the tail when not in use. The male typically mounts the female from the rear. Fertilization is internal. Females of most species are able to store viable sperm for a period of one to five years. All turtles lay eggs. The eggs are characteristically laid on land in a hole dug by the female with her rear feet in moist earth or sand. A female may lay eggs several times a year to every few years, depending on the individual and the reproductive strategy of the particular species. The number of eggs deposited varies with the individual species. Incubation may take $1\frac{1}{2}$ to 9 months, again, depending on the species as well as the temperature and humidity in the nest hole. Many turtles have temperature-dependent sex determination (TSD) of offspring; that is, the specific incubation temperatures will establish whether the young will be males or females.

Turtles have a potentially long life span. Under ideal conditions, many have a life expectancy of 50 to 80 years. Individuals of some species, including many land tortoises, are capable of surviving for over a century.

The terms "turtle" and "tortoise" may be used differently in several of the English-speaking countries. In the United States, the vernacular name "turtle" refers to all chelonians, while "tortoise" is synonymous with land turtle and should only be applied to members of Family Testudinidae, which typically have elephant-like rear legs, toes without webbing, and a domed carapace.

Turtles are divided into two main groups by taxonomists, depending on the way the neck is retracted into the shell. Turtles that fold their necks to the side when withdrawing their heads are collectively categorized as Pleurodira (sidenecks and snakenecks) while turtles that pull their necks straight back are classified as Cryptodira. All turtles occurring in the Hawaiian Islands or its surrounding seas belong to the Cryptodira.

SEMIAQUATIC FRESHWATER TURTLES
Family Emydidae

Of 257 total species of turtles found worldwide, 94 belong to Family Emydidae (Iverson, 1992). Representative emydid species are widespread in North America and occur also in Central and South America, Europe, Asia, including Japan, and North Africa. Members of this family typically have relatively small heads, a low-arched carapace, a broad bridge between the carapace and plastron, and a neck that is retracted directly back into the shell rather than folded back in a sideways manner.

Red-eared Slider
(Trachemys scripta elegans)

Red-eared Slider, *Trachemys scripta elegans.*

Identification: The Red-eared Slider is a medium-sized 5 to 10 in. (12.5 to 25 cm) turtle that is instantly recognizable by a prominent patch of red on each side of the head behind the eye. The carapace of this turtle is olive green or brown with dark markings on each scute or shield. The plastron is light-colored with one dark blotch on each scute. The chin has narrow yellow stripes. Old individuals, especially males, are often darker and the eye stripe may be more obscure.

These turtles live in ponds, drainage ditches and freshwater sloughs which have slow-running water, shoreline vegetation cover, and a muddy bottom. The common name "slider" comes from this turtle's habit of "sliding off" logs and stumps into the water at the first sign of danger.

Juvenile Red-eared Slider.

Distribution: Native to the Mississippi Valley of North America, it naturally occurs from as far north as Illinois to the Gulf of Mexico. Hatchling and juvenile Red-eared Sliders have been exported by the hundreds of thousands to other areas of the United States and abroad for the pet trade. An extremely hardy turtle, this species has established breeding populations in a number of

Red-eared slider.

places outside its natural range as far away as Asia and Europe. Wild Hawaiian specimens are the result of fish pond escapees and also turtles that outgrew their living quarters and were released by their well-intentioned owners into the wild. While these turtles are present in a number of waterways on O'ahu and Kaua'i, the only reproducing population the author has observed is in the large Kawai Nui marsh and accompanying drainage ditches including Ka'elepulu stream inland from Kailua, on the windward side of O'ahu. Hatchlings and juveniles have routinely been observed there during the 1980s and 1990s.

Reproduction: Within its natural range, courtship and mating take place in the spring and fall. Males are typically smaller than females and, in addition, have a longer, thicker tail, and longer, slightly curved front claws. During courtship, the male swims in front of the female, extends his forelimbs and strokes the female's face with his claws. Both courtship and mating take place in the water. If the female is receptive, the male mounts from the rear and the pair sink to the bottom to copulate. The female Red-eared Slider digs a flask-shaped nest hole alternately using her rear feet. Several clutches of two to 25 oval-shaped, thin-shelled white eggs may be laid during the year. Incubation usually takes between 60 and 75 days. As is the case with most other turtle species, the sex of each Red-eared Slider will be determined by the incubation temperatures that the eggs are exposed to during incubation. Hatchlings and small juveniles are round in appearance. Hatchlings have a green carapace with yellow marks, the distinctive red eye stripe, and are $1^3/_{16}$–$1^5/_{16}$ in. (30–33 mm) in length. Newly hatched juveniles are carnivorous, feeding on aquatic invertebrates including aquatic worms and snails as well as small fish and tadpoles. As they grow larger, they feed on more and more plant material. Adult "Red-ears" are omnivorous.

Interesting Fact: Red-eared Slider hatchlings, sold locally as pets in the islands in the old days, were called "coin turtles," both because they were thought to bring good luck, and because they were the size of several U.S. silver coins.

Care in Captivity: Turtles in general are not well-suited to living indoors unless the potential owners have advanced aquarium experience with exotics. Rather, Red-eared Sliders should be maintained in an outdoor pond within a fenced enclosure to prevent escapes. Live plants are essential. Small juveniles will take live tubifex worms and feeder guppies. Larger juveniles and adults will feed on trout chow, feeder guppies and goldfish as well as a variety of aquatic plants. The pond and enclosure must be kept clean. Any food not eaten must be removed. Rotting food dramatically increases the chances of the turtles developing and carrying *Salmonella*. These *Salmonella* organisms can be transferred to people, causing severe diarrhea. It is important that small children routinely wash their hands with soap and water after handling turtles and before putting their hands in their mouths. These routine precautions normally prevent salmonellosis, should it in fact be present, from being transferred to humans.

SOFTSHELL TURTLES
Family Trionychidae

Softshell turtles are leathery-skinned freshwater chelonians whose rounded, flattened shells have reduced bony scutes or plates. These turtles, which have a broad geographic range worldwide, have been described by one expert as "animated pancakes." There are 22 living species in this family. All have long, retractile necks, snorkel-like snouts and paddlelike limbs, each with three claws. Softshells are quite shy of man, and are quick, agile swimmers. Both species in Hawai'i, which are of Asian origin, are more aquatic than North American mainland species and rarely come out of the water during the day. Interestingly, studies by Bull and Vogt (1979) indicate that there is no temperature-dependent sex determination (TSD) in softshell turtles.

Wattle-necked Softshell Turtle
(Palea steindachneri)

Wattle-necked Softshell Turtle, *Palea steindachneri*.

The Wattle-necked Softshell Turtle has keen senses of sight and hearing. It is adapted to an aquatic life, swims well, and can hold its breath underwater for over an hour. It is established in some of the streams, canals, freshwater marshes, ponds and drainage ditches on the islands of Kaua'i and O'ahu, and is the more common of the two species of softshells on the Islands. These softshell turtles were sometimes propagated locally in fish ponds. Few local people are aware of the presence of this reptile because it is almost entirely

Frontal close-up of Wattle-necked Softshell Turtle.

aquatic and rarely comes out of the water to bask. The typical specimen donated to the Honolulu Zoo was initially mistaken for "a rock on the bottom of the stream that moved when I stepped on it."

Wattle-necked Softshell Turtles are opportunistic and primarily carnivorous, feeding on fish, crayfish, mollusks and bullfrogs. One specimen was observed partially eating a large

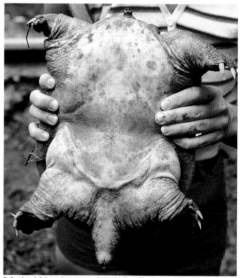

Male Wattle-necked Softshell Turtle, ventral view; note lack of patterned plastron.

Hatchling Wattle-necked Softshell Turtle, ventral view.

Giant Toad, leaving intact and not consuming the head, upper back including the parotoid glands, and legs. It suffered no ill effects from this incident. These turtles can grow to a length of about 16 inches (41 cm). Males gen-

Wattle-necked Softshell Turtle, *Palea steindachneri.*

Hatchling Wattle-necked Softshell Turtle.

erally have considerably longer tails, with the vent opening closer to the tail tip. Adults are territorial and may be aggressive towards others of the same species in a confined area.

Identification: The Wattle-necked Softshell Turtle can be distinguished from the Chinese Softshell Turtle dorsally by the presence of a clump of tubercles (wattles) where the front of the shell joins the neck. Hatchlings have a light yellow neck stripe and light yellow markings on the throat. These fade within the first year. Ventrally, neonates are a lemon yellow color and lack a plastral pattern. Adults have a gray ventral surface with pinkish mottling and also lack a plastral pattern. In contrast, the Chinese Softshell Turtle lacks the dorsal tubercles and always has a patterned plastron. Red-eared Sliders, which are present in some Hawaiian waterways, do not have leathery, pliable shells.

Distribution: These turtles are found in streams, freshwater marshes, ponds, reservoirs and canals on the islands of Oʻahu and Kauaʻi. This turtle is native to China including Kwangtung, Kwangsi, and Hainan Island. It is also present in Vietnam.

Reproduction: Mating occurs in the water. Eggs are deposited in moist soil above the water line. The female digs a hole with her hind feet about 4 in. (10.2 cm) across and 4–5 in. (10.2–12.7 cm) deep. She deposits her eggs and then fills in the hole. Clutch size varies from three to 28. The round white eggs average about $^7/_8$ in. (22 mm) in diameter. The eggs have an incubation period of 48–68 days. A female may lay between one and four clutches a year. The young are about one in. (2.5 cm) long upon hatching. They resemble the adults except for the presence of tiny dorsal tubercles on the shell and a yellow neck stripe which disappear with age. Sexual maturity is reached during the fifth or sixth year. This turtle is not aggressive. However, if captured and handled carelessly, it is capable of giving a painful bite.

Interesting Fact: Chinese immigrants first came to Hawaiʻi to work in the 1850s. They brought a number of live animals for food with them. Different releases probably occurred both before and after 1900. It is known that softshells also used to be imported from the Orient alive, as an item of food prior to World War II.

Care in Captivity: These turtles are only suitably maintained in a large, outdoor fish pond, the bottom and sides of which should be smooth. Rough surfaces such as lava rock can cause damage to the underside of the feet and to the shell. The pool must be kept clean and hygienic. Additionally, there should be a smooth sloping side at one end with a sand or earth haul-out area which can also double as an egg-laying site. Feed appropriately-sized whole fresh fish. Hatchlings will take live tubifex worms and feeder guppies.

Chinese Softshell Turtle
(Pelodiscus sinensis)

Chinese Softshell Turtle, *Pelodiscus sinensis.*

A mid-sized, grayish softshell turtle, it is found in canals, streams, ponds, drainage ditches and freshwater marshes. Like the Wattle-necked Softshell, it probably arrived with Chinese and Japanese immigrants during the mid- to late 1800s and was also imported live as a food item until the beginning of

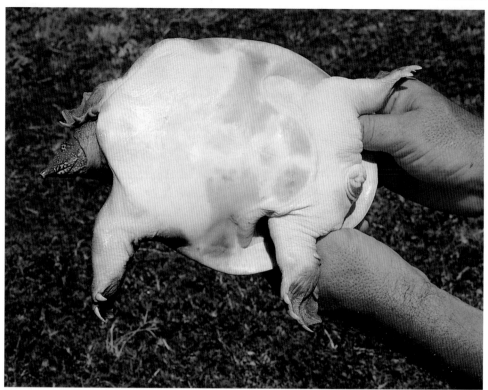

Chinese Softshell Turtle, female; ventral view showing patterned plastron.

World War II. This turtle is primarily carnivorous, feeding on freshwater vertebrates and invertebrates. Chinese Softshells may bite if handled carelessly.

Identification: The Chinese Softshell Turtle lacks the clump of tubercles at the front of the shell of the Wattle-necked Softshell. Tiny dark spots are present on the head and neck. The ventral surface is whitish with a distinct pattern present. Hatchlings and small juveniles can be easily distinguished from hatchling Wattle-necked Softshells by the absence of a yellow neck stripe.

Distribution: Chinese Softshells naturally occur in southern and central China, including the island of Hainan, in Vietnam and are also present in Taiwan. They have been introduced into Japan, Timor, and at least one of the Bonin Islands. They are the less common of the two introduced Asian softshells found on the Hawaiian Islands of Kaua'i and O'ahu.

Reproduction: Mating occurs in the water. The gravid female will dig a nest on land above the waterline when she is ready to lay. The eggs are white and spherical in shape. Eggs average about $3/4$ to 1 in. (22 to 25 mm) in size. Clutch size has been documented at 15–28 eggs, with multiple clutches being laid during the year. Depending on the incubation temperatures, the eggs take 40–80 days to hatch. Hatchlings average slightly over 1 in. (27 mm) in length.

Habitat of Softshell Turtles in Hawai'i. Here the author is accompanied in the field by University of Hawai'i, Hilo biogeographer and turtle specialist Dr. James O. Juvik.

Interesting Fact: Hatchling and juvenile softshells benefit from being maintained in their own outdoor enclosures which offer both sun and shade. Some exposure to the ultraviolet rays of the sun is essential. When juveniles are housed indoors, fungal and bacterial infections of the shell frequently occur and do not typically respond to antibiotic treatment. These may lead to the demise of the young turtles.

Eggs of a Chinese Softshell Turtle.

Care in Captivity: Use the same care instructions as for the Wattle-necked Softshell Turtle *(Palea steindachneri)*.

HEAD SHIELDS OF SEA TURTLES KEY

S. McKeown

GREEN SEA TURTLE

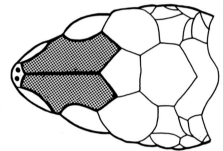

1 pair of prefrontal
shields

HAWKSBILL TURTLE

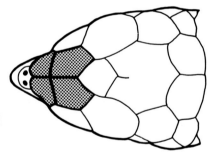

2 pairs of prefrontal
shields

© *Drawings by Wesley Chun*

MARINE TURTLES

There are five species of marine turtles which may be found in the seas around Hawai'i. All are air-breathing reptiles with long, paddle-shaped limbs referred to as flippers and are especially adapted to life in the ocean. All migrate great distances across the open seas and all must return to land to lay their eggs. Not much is known about the lives of juvenile sea turtles. It is known, however, that adult marine turtles migrate from their regular ocean feeding grounds to their nesting beaches. Reproductively active adults return to mate in the water. Females come ashore to lay their eggs on the same beaches on which they were born. In past centuries, sea turtles were much more common in and around most of the Pacific islands and were an important food source to the Polynesians, especially for important feasts. However, due to the tremendous exploitation by man during the 19th and 20th centuries for meat, soup, leather, and shell artifacts, the world's sea turtle populations have declined dramatically, and several species are in danger of extinction in many parts of their range. All sea turtles belong either to the Family Cheloniidae or Dermochelidae. The sex of the offspring of sea turtles is determined by the temperatures at which their eggs incubate.

SEA TURTLES
Family Cheloniidae

Sea turtles of this family are mid- to large-sized with paddle-shaped limbs and hard, plate-covered, heart- or shield-shaped shells. Most rarely venture onto land except to nest. Four species are found in the seas around the Hawaiian Islands: the Pacific Green Sea Turtle *(Chelonia mydas agassizii)*, the Pacific Hawksbill Sea Turtle *(Eretmochelys imbricata bissa),* the Olive Ridley Sea Turtle *(Lepidochelys olivacea),* and the Loggerhead Sea Turtle *(Caretta caretta).*

Pacific Green Sea Turtle
(Chelonia mydas agassizii)

Pacific Green Sea Turtle.

The Pacific Green Sea Turtle ("Honu" in Hawaiian) is the most prevalent marine turtle in the seas around Hawai'i. This shy, gentle, 150–400 lb. (68–180 kg) air-breathing reptile is primarily herbivorous, grazing in shallow waters on algae or limu (seaweed) or other marine vegetation that grows in underwater "pastures" in waters surrounding the Hawaiian Islands. Its carapace may be dark olive, dark brown, or grayish-black with yellow streaking. The plastron is light yellow or orangish. The word "green" in its name refers not to the color of the skin or shell, but rather to the greenish color of the fat inside its body. Turtle soup is derived from the cartilage or "calipee" in the turtle's plastron. It is the vegetarian diet of adults of this species that gives its flesh and cartilage an excellent flavor. Man is the turtle's deadliest enemy. Over-exploitation of both eggs and adult animals within the past 150 years has resulted in serious population declines locally and around the world.

Identification: Adults from Hawaiian waters have a shell length ranging from 32–42 in. (81–107 cm). Unlike the Hawksbill Sea Turtle, the large scutes of the carapace do *not* overlap and there is only a *single* pair of prefrontal scales on the head between the eyes. (See Head Shields of Sea Turtles Key.) Hatchlings differ from other sea turtles by having a white plastron that sharply contrasts with the dark-colored carapace. However, Hawaiian specimens develop black pigment at two to three weeks of age which dissipates and becomes white again at about four to five months of age.

Distribution: This turtle is found in tropical and subtropical waters of the Pacific and Indian Oceans. In Hawai'i, adults of both sexes commonly come ashore during the day to bask on the uninhabited "Leeward" or Northwestern Hawaiian Islands.

Pacific Green Sea Turtle laying eggs at French Frigate Shoals.

Reproduction: Between May and August, adult Green Sea Turtles from Hawaiian waters migrate up to 800 mi. (1,290 km) primarily to French Frigate Shoals, although a small number travel to other parts of the uninhabited Leeward or Northwestern Islands that extend for approximately 1,000 mi. (1,600 km) northwest of Kaua'i. These tiny, isolated volcanic islands, coral reefs, and shoals, first set aside as a wildlife sanctuary in 1909, are today known as the Hawaiian Islands National Wildlife Refuge. There, adult Green Sea Turtles mate in the water. The males may be identified by their much longer, thicker tails. During mating, the male uses his flippers to grasp the female's shell to hold her in place. Females crawl ashore at night, up to several times during each breeding season. Once a nest site has been selected, the female, initially using her front flippers and then alternately using her hind flippers, digs out a nest in the sand well above the high-tide mark. The female lays anywhere from 50 to 150 eggs, after which she carefully fills in the hole. The entire laying process is laborious and may last into the early morning. When finished, the female returns to the sea. The eggs incubate for 50–60 days and all the hatchlings emerge within a short time of one another. The baby Green Sea Turtles, each about 2 in. (5.1 cm) in length, race for the ocean immediately after emerging from the nest. At French Frigate Shoals, unlike some nesting beaches in other parts of the world, seabirds generally do not eat the young, but they are easy pickings for crabs and reef fish. Few will

Pacific Green Sea Turtle with viral tumor disease.

Juvenile Green Sea Turtle, *Chelonia mydas agassizii.*

Pacific Green Sea Turtle resting next to a Hawaiian Monk Seal during the day on one of the Leeward Islands.

Hatchling Pacific Green Sea Turtle.

survive the rigors of the next two to three decades to return to the same beach as nesting adults.

Small numbers of Green Sea Turtles still reproduce on N.W. Moloka'i. In earlier times, this species also nested at Polihua, a white sand beach on the northern shore of Lana'i. However, overkilling of turtles during the early 1900s essentially destroyed this population of nesting adults.

Protected Status: Since 1978, the Pacific Green Sea Turtle has been classified as threatened in Hawaiian waters under the Endangered Species Act by the United States Department of Commerce and the United States Department of the Interior and may not be taken or killed. All sea turtles are also protected under Hawai'i state law. This combined protection has resulted in many less sea turtles being killed for food and this species is now more common in Hawaiian waters and reefs than it was in recent past decades.

Special note: Tragically, at a number of sites worldwide, Green Sea Turtles have been affected by a suspected viral disease known as fibropapillomatosis.

This disease, uncommon before 1985, is characterized by tumors that affect the internal organs, and which also develop on the turtle's flippers, neck, eyes and head. If these tumors grow to where they cover the eyes, the turtles typically stop feeding and frequently starve to death. In Hawaiian waters, the presence of these tumors varies from locality to locality. Perhaps 50% of the Green Sea Turtles in Kane'ohe Bay on O'ahu have the disease, about 35% of those off Moloka'i have it, while other areas such as the waters off the Kona Coast of the Big Island are free of it for now. Additionally, Green Sea Turtles with fibropapillomas are sometimes heavily parasitized on these damaged areas of skin by marine leeches. We can only hope that ongoing research on this turtle tumor disease will lead to a possible vaccine and a cure for these gentle marine reptiles.

Pacific Hawksbill Sea Turtle
(Eretmochelys imbricata bissa)

Pacific Hawksbill Sea Turtle, *Eretmochelys imbricata bissa.*

The Pacific Hawksbill Sea Turtle ("'Ea" or "Honu'ea" in Hawaiian), while still the second most prevalent marine turtle in Hawaiian waters, is now extremely uncommon. A mid-sized sea turtle, it has an average shell length of 32 in. (81 cm) and an average weight of 75 to 150 lb. (34 to 68 kg). The shell is shield-shaped, generally mottled-brown above and yellow below. Commercial "tortoiseshell" or "carey," from the shell plates of this turtle used to be

Pacific Hawksbill Sea Turtle, ventral view.

extracted from Hawksbills slaughtered solely for the manufacture of combs, brushes, buttons, and similar items before the development of plastics. Exploitation outside the United States occurs even today, despite the fact that the turtle is technically protected by international law.

The Hawksbill feeds primarily on sponges. Crabs, sea urchins, fish, shellfish, jellyfish and seaweed may also occasionally be consumed. When feeding on jellyfish, it closes its eyes to protect them from the stinging tentacles. The narrow hawk-like beak, from which this species derives its common name, is well-adapted to probing into holes in the coral reef in search of food. Since its flesh can be toxic because of its diet, Hawksbills historically have not been eaten in the Hawaiian Islands.

Identification: The distinctive pointed snout easily distinguishes it from all other marine turtles. Also, the Hawksbill differs from the Green Sea Turtle in having *two* pairs of prefrontal scales on its head instead of just one pair. (See Head Shields of Sea Turtles Key.) The dorsal plates (laminae) strongly overlap. Also, the edges of the carapace are clearly serrated in juvenile and subadult specimens. Adult hawksbills do not reach the

Pacific Hawksbill Sea Turtle, nesting female.

large size of fully mature Green Sea Turtles. Hatchlings are brownish-black above and black below.

Distribution: Although found in tropical oceans worldwide, this species is becoming increasingly rare.

Reproduction: Reproductively active adult Hawksbills migrate to and mate in the ocean off the nesting beach. Each gravid female comes ashore at night, digs a deep hole in the sand above the high water mark with her rear flippers, and lays 125 to 175 perfectly round, white eggs. She covers the hole and laboriously makes her way back to the relative safety of the water. The eggs usually hatch in 53 to 74 (average 59) days. Nestings in the Hawaiian Islands are relatively uncommon and typically only occur on the Big Island (Hawai'i) and on Moloka'i. Very recently there have been one or two nestings recorded each year on Maui. Nesting typically takes place on black sand and gravel beaches on these islands.

Special Note: This species is listed as endangered under the U.S. Endangered Species Act and is also listed under Appendix I of CITES. It may not be taken in Hawaiian waters for any purpose except by permit for valid research (e.g., tagging, etc.).

Olive Ridley Sea Turtle
(Lepidochelys olivacea)

Olive Ridley Sea Turtle, *Lepidochelys olivacea.*

The Olive Ridley Sea Turtle is the smallest marine turtle that ranges into Hawaiian waters. An adult weighs only 80 to 100 lbs. (36–45 kg) and attains a

Olive Ridley Sea Turtle, ventral view.

size of about 2 ft. (58–74 cm) in length. It is not common in the seas around Hawai'i. However, it occasionally occurs as a stray, probably originating from the eastern Pacific, off Mexico and Central America.

Identification: It is distinguished by its overall relatively small size and rounded or heart-shaped, light olive-gray carapace that is dorsally flattened and serrated along its posterior margin. Both the bridge and plastron are greenish-white or light greenish-yellow. The skin is an olive color above and lighter below. Its dorsal plates (scutes) do not overlap. The only sea turtle it resembles in the Pacific, the Loggerhead, is much larger, with a rather elongate reddish-brown carapace. Also, the three or four large bridge scutes on the Loggerhead **lack** pores.

Distribution: The Olive Ridley lives in tropical portions of the Pacific and Indian Oceans from India, Micronesia, Japan and Arabia south to Australia and South Africa. It is present in the eastern Pacific from California south to the Galapagos Islands as well. It is also wide ranging in warmer parts of the Atlantic and occurs in the Caribbean. While Pacific and Atlantic populations may be distinct, no subspecies are currently recognized.

Reproduction: Like other sea turtles, males have long, thick tails and some concavity of the plastron. Males also have a well-developed, curved claw on each front flipper which assists in holding the female in place in the water during mating. Nestings occur on a number of beaches in both the northern and southern hemispheres. Females in egg-laying cycles typically nest twice (less frequently three times) a season. The size of each clutch may vary between 30 and 168 eggs. The incubation period is 50–70 days.

Only one nesting involving a single female has been documented for the Pacific Ridley in Hawai'i. That nesting took place on a beach in the Paeahu area of Maui during September, 1985.

Interesting Fact: When Ridleys are ready to nest, it is common for great numbers of females to come ashore at the same time with the rising tide in the late afternoon to lay their eggs. These unique reproductive efforts are known as arribadas. Nesting arribadas of over 100,000 females have been recorded at a beach near Orissa, India. Key nesting areas are thus quite vulnerable to exploitation by humans. Fortunately, some of these beaches now receive protection.

Protected Status: In Hawaiian waters, this species is listed as threatened under the U.S. Endangered Species Act. It is also protected under category I of CITES.

Loggerhead Sea Turtle
(Caretta caretta)

Loggerhead Sea Turtle, *Caretta caretta*.

The Loggerhead is the single living member of its genus. It is a large sea turtle, averaging 31–45 in. (79–114 cm); record 84 in. (213 cm) in length. It attains a weight of 170–350 lbs. (77–159 kg); record 500+ lbs. (227+ kg).

This marine reptile is primarily carnivorous, feeding on sponges, jellyfish, clams, sea urchins, and fishes. It is occasionally found far out to sea, although it typically feeds among coral reefs and occasionally enters coastal salt marshes and bays.

Identification: The head is large, the snout short and rounded. The posterior portion of the head is broad and the neck quite stout. Two claws are present on each forelimb. The reddish-brown carapace is somewhat elongate. The individual scutes may be bordered with yellow. The carapace is highest anteriorly and is serrated towards the rear. The number of costals on each side of the carapace is usually five, rarely four, and the first always touches the nuchal plate. Three to four large, poreless scutes are present on the bridge between the carapace and plastron. In subadult specimens, a middorsal keel is present. Juveniles are brown above and lighter below. Three dorsal keels and two plastral keels are evident in juveniles. Hatchlings average $1^5/_8$–$1^7/_8$ in. (41–48 mm) in length.

Similar species: The Olive Ridley is significantly smaller with a more circular, olive-gray carapace and with pored scutes on the bridge. Unlike the Green Sea Turtle and Hawksbill Sea Turtle, the first costal plate does **not** touch the nuchal plate.

Distribution: The Loggerhead inhabits the Pacific, Indian and Atlantic oceans. Specimens that are thought to originate from the seas around Japan occasionally come into Hawaiian waters, but egg-laying has not been documented on the Hawaiian Islands.

Reproduction: Males can be distinguished from females by a more tapering shell and a much longer and thicker tail. The Loggerhead, like other sea turtles, may travel great distances between its feeding grounds and laying beaches. Mating takes place in the ocean off the nesting beaches. During copulation, the male holds the female in place by grasping the edges of her carapace with the claws on each front and hind flipper. As with other sea turtles, during mating the male may nip the female's neck. His long tail is angled down under hers so that his penis can be inserted into her cloaca. The female may accept or attempt to resist. Like all sea turtles, paired adults may copulate for hours at a time.

Nestings for Pacific Ocean populations have been recorded from Japan, Australia and Fiji. Most nestings take place in the spring or early summer. The females come ashore at night to dig their nests above the high tide mark. Reproductively active females may nest several times a year, often at intervals of every 12 to 15 days. Nesting is cyclical and does not take place every year.

When the female finds a suitable nesting site, she first digs out a recessed area around her body, referred to as a "body pit," and then, using her hind feet, digs a nest cavity 6–10 in. (15–25 cm) deep. The leathery-shelled eggs are spherical and approximately $1^7/_{16}$–$1^{15}/_{16}$ in. (35–49 mm). A female may lay between 64 and 150 eggs. Incubation can vary between 49 and 73 days. As with most turtles, the sex of the offspring is determined by the egg incubation

Loggerhead Sea Turtle, *Caretta caretta*.

temperatures. With the Loggerhead, eggs incubated at a temperature of 82°F (28°C) or less will produce all males. Eggs which incubate between 82 and 90°F (28 and 32°C) will yield offspring of both sexes, while eggs incubated at temperatures of 90°F (32°C) or slightly higher will produce all females.

Hatchlings of this species typically emerge at night and immediately make their way to the water. Few hatchlings survive the many predators to reach adulthood.

Protected Status: This species of sea turtle is listed as threatened under the U.S. Endangered Species Act and under Appendix I of CITES. It is fully protected and may not be taken in Hawaiian waters.

Interesting Fact: Adult Loggerheads and other sea turtles are highly susceptible to being drowned in shrimp boat trawling nets. A federal law now requires shrimpers to use turtle excluder devices (TEDS). Some shrimpers do not obey the law. Also, some fishermen with large nets operate them improperly, thus drowning sea turtles. If you should witness any of these highly unethical (and illegal) practices, report them immediately to the enforcement division of the regional office of the National Marine Fisheries Service, U.S. Fish and Wildlife Service (USFWS), or state fisheries enforcement authorities.

LEATHERBACK SEA TURTLES
Family Dermochelyidae

The Family Dermochelyidae is represented by only a single living species. This reptile, the Leatherback Sea Turtle, is easily distinguished from other marine turtles by having seven distinctive longitudinal ridges running the entire length of the body. Additionally, it lacks a hard, bony scute-covered shell and is, instead, covered with layers of smooth, black skin.

Pacific Leatherback Sea Turtle
(Dermochelys coriacea schlegelii)

Pacific Leatherback Sea Turtle, *Dermochelys coriacea schlegelii.*

The Pacific Leatherback Sea Turtle is the largest of all living turtles, frequently weighing between 700 and 1,400 lbs. (315 and 630 kg), with a record weight of approximately 1,500 lbs. (680 kg). It attains a length of 5 to 7 ft. (1.5–2.1 m), with a record size of approximately 8 ft. (2.4 m). This is the only marine turtle that does not have a "typical" hard turtle shell. Instead, it has a covering of smooth leathery skin set over a layer of small irregular bones. There are seven pronounced longitudinal ridges on the dorsal surface and five more on its underside. This marine turtle has massive flippers.

The Leatherback is the fastest and most powerful of any of the sea turtles and can swim at speeds in excess of 19 mi. (30 km) per hour. It is pelagic; that is, it lives in the open ocean in deep water and usually at a considerable distance from land. Although rare, there is hope for its survival in that only its

Pacific Leatherback Turtle, hatchling.

Pacific Leatherback Sea Turtle, close-up of head and neck.

eggs are generally exploited by man. Its meat is oily and poor-tasting, and its body has little economic value.

Identification: This turtle has a leathery shell. It is the only sea turtle that **lacks claws** along the anterior edge of its flippers. Adults are black with light-colored spots on the head, back and limbs. The plastron of the male is concave, the posterior portion of the shell is more tapered and the tail is over twice as long as that of the female. Hatchlings are slate gray or black with white or yellow spotting.

Distribution: The local subspecies of the Leatherback is wide-ranging in tropical and temperate waters of the Pacific and Indian Oceans. While nesting in the tropics, it migrates seasonally during the warmer months to the cold, temperate seas in search of jellyfish blooms. The Leatherback is occasionally found in deep water off the Hawaiian Islands.

If approached or attacked by a shark, a Leatherback may, for defense, act aggressively by swimming towards the shark, then surfacing and somersaulting over backwards, creating a frothy wake of bubbles. It continues its erratic behavior until the confused shark swims away.

Reproduction: This huge marine reptile is not known to nest in Hawai'i but regularly occurs in the surrounding seas. It has been recorded as nesting on beaches in Malaysia, South Africa, New Guinea, Australia, Mexico and at several other locations. A female will lay 50 to 170 eggs in a hole she has dug above the high-water mark on a sandy beach. The eggs are spherical and $1^{7}/_{8}$–$2^{1}/_{2}$ in. (49–65 mm) in diameter. Incubation takes 53–74 days. Hatchlings are a mere $2^{1}/_{4}$–$2^{1}/_{2}$ in. (56–63 mm) long and have an outer layer of scales that are shed within the first month of life. Very little is known about the habits of partially grown adults. Both young and adults feed primarily on jellyfish. Squid, octopi, sea urchins, crustaceans, and floating seaweed are also sometimes consumed.

Protected Status: The Pacific Leatherback Sea Turtle is listed as endangered worldwide by the U.S. Department of the Interior and Commerce and is on Appendix I of CITES. It may not be taken in Hawaiian waters.

Interesting Fact: Reptiles are typically ectothermic. Unlike other reptiles and all other turtles, the Leatherback Sea Turtle is considered functionally endothermic. While this endothermic ability partially derives from its huge size and associated slower heat loss, its oil-rich skin provides insulation as well. Additionally, the circulatory, counter-flow system in its limbs acts to conserve body heat.

The Brown Tree Snake *(Boiga irregularis)* Threat To Hawai'i

Brown Tree Snake, *Boiga irregularis, in Guam.*

This rear-fanged, mildly venomous arboreal snake can live in virtually any habitat — natural, disturbed or manmade. On Guam, where it was accidentally introduced in the mid- to late 1940s, it is commonly found in both wet and dry forest, grassy fields, livestock areas, gardens, garages and roofs of homes. The Brown Tree Snake remains out of sight during the day curled up in tree crevices, under debris, rocks or in holes in the ground. At night, it becomes active, leaving its hiding place in search of food. Its principal diet is birds and their eggs, small mammals, and lizards. If startled, it will strike aggressively. Its thin body shape and light weight allows it to strike a greater distance than most snakes. It has an effective strike range of over half the length of its body.

Identification: Very distinctive in appearance, this species is characterized by a broad, flattened head, extremely large eyes that are yellowish with a dark vertical-shaped pupil. The neck and body are thin, and the tail is long. There are 19–23 mid-body scale rows and the scales are smooth. The ventral anal scale is undivided. Typically, this snake is rust colored, reddish-brown, brown, or light brown with numerous irregular lines, bars or blotches running across the body. Some dorsal scales may be edged with black. It can grow to over ten ft. (3 m) in length.

Reproduction: This is an egg-laying species. Between four and twelve oblong leathery eggs are deposited in hollow logs, in crevices, under debris, or other sites where the eggs are protected from desiccation and high temperatures. Females may produce up to two clutches a year. Both the number and timing of clutches may depend on prey abundance and seasonal variation in climate. It may be possible for female Brown Tree Snakes to store sperm and produce fertile eggs for several years after a successful mating. However, the reproductive characteristics of this snake are still not well known.

Distribution: The Brown Tree Snake is native to the South Pacific island of New Guinea and nearby smaller islands as well as parts of Indonesia. A similar, smaller form occurs in northern and eastern Australia. The Brown Tree Snake is now widely distributed on the Micronesian island of Guam. This species is thought to have arrived in Guam by stowing away on military cargo transferred from New Guinea or Manus Island off New Guinea by the U.S. military during or directly following World War II. Guam is a U.S. territory located 3,700 mi. (5,950 km) southwest of Hawai'i and 1,500 mi. (2,410 km) southeast of Japan. Guam is about 30 mi. (50 km) long. It has extensive U.S. military bases and flight lines staffed by U.S. military personnel with tens of thousands of U.S. military dependents living off-base as well. Military and commercial flights and the transfer of supplies and cargo regularly occur between Guam and the Hawaiian Islands. It is common to find these snakes on runways and around ship container freight storage areas on Guam at night. They sometimes crawl into plane wheel wells or cargo areas. To date, less than ten Brown Tree Snakes have turned up in Hawai'i, all on airport runways or in cargo storage areas. **At this time (1996), the Brown Tree Snake is not believed to be established on the Hawaiian Islands.** Its presence would be an ecological disaster were it to gain a foothold in Hawai'i.

On Guam, this snake is responsible for the disappearance of most of the birdlife on that island, including the extinction of a number of endemic bird species. Also, Brown Tree Snakes are responsible for several hundred power outages on Guam each year by crawling up telephone poles and onto electric transformers and shorting them out. The damage to electrical systems and perishable goods because of the resulting power outages has been in the millions of dollars.

Interesting Fact: Brown Tree Snakes are **not** typical of snakes in general. The great majority of snakes are non-venomous and harmless to humans. Virtually all other snakes are specialized as to where they can live and what they can eat. Most snakes feed on mice and rats and benefit mankind. Brown Tree Snakes do not benefit humans. Brown Tree Snakes can live anywhere and eat almost any vertebrate animal that can be swallowed. Almost all other species of land snakes occur in low densities throughout most of the year. Brown Tree Snakes occur in very high densities year-round. No other snake has caused the extinction of a single species of animal anywhere in the world. Other snakes have difficulty living around places that people inhabit. Brown Tree Snakes around human dwellings at least as well as in natural, undisturbed areas. Virtually all snakes are attracted by the movement of a particular prey species which they eat. In contrast, Brown Tree Snakes can also be attracted by the smell of blood or other odors. Virtually no snakes attempt to eat human infants (or humans); large Brown Tree Snakes may try to consume infants. These comparisons demonstrate how different Brown Tree Snakes are from other snakes.

A common fallacy in Hawai'i is that Brown Tree Snakes might enter the state as people's pets from places other than Guam. This simply is not the case. Brown Tree Snakes are not kept as pets on the U.S. mainland. All Brown Tree Snakes that have turned up in Hawai'i have been unwanted stowaways off military planes, civilian planes and ship container freight from Guam. The way to keep Brown Tree Snakes out of Hawai'i is to follow a strict protocol regarding movement for all cargo and supplies, military household items and military equipment from Guam to Hawai'i. Much of that protocol is now in place. It needs to continue to be funded, actively supported, rigorously enforced, and expanded. Sniffer dogs are **essential** for checking all personal luggage, cargo, supplies, container freight and aircraft moving between Guam and Hawai'i, both before departure and upon arrival. Hawai'i's endemic birds and other wildlife are at risk if Brown Tree Snakes ever become established in Hawai'i.

Care in Captivity: The Brown Tree Snake is not suitable to keep as a pet. It is rear-fanged and venomous, although not generally regarded as deadly to humans. Large fines and a jail sentence await anyone with a captive Brown Tree Snake in the Hawaiian Islands, and rightly so. Any snake casually encountered in the wild in Hawai'i that is suspected of being a Brown Tree Snake should be immediately (but safely) captured and turned over to the Hawai'i State Dept. of Agriculture with accompanying location/capture data.

Island Supertramp Species

I have coined the term "island supertramp" to describe an animal that, upon becoming established in an island environment in which it is not native, does major irrevocable damage to the fauna or flora where it has been introduced. Although a number of species can become established outside their natural range, only a tiny percentage of animals worldwide can be considered potential island supertramps.

Island ecosystems are fragile and are especially susceptible to damage, so every effort must be made to keep island supertramps out or, if they are already present on one island, to limit their distribution so they do not spread to other islands.

Rats are probably the most damaging animals introduced by modern man into the Hawaiian Islands before 1900. The most destructive supertramp species established in Hawai'i in this century are bulbuls. Bulbuls are highly aggressive Southeast Asian birds which push other birds in Hawai'i out of their

Brown Tree Snake, an island supertramp species in Guam.

territories and outcompete them for food. Bulbuls work together in pairs or family groups. These birds also damage fruit and orchid crops, and eat large quantities of endemic insects including fruit flies as well as small lizards. Red-vented Bulbuls can be described as "avian Brown Tree Snakes" or "flying rats." In the mere 30 years since their illegal introduction, they have become one of the two or three most common bird species on Oʻahu. Every effort must be made to prevent their spread to neighboring islands to ensure Hawaiʻi's continued biodiversity.

The development of an "island supertramp task force" by the appropriate governmental

Red-vented Bulbul, an island supertramp species in Hawaii.

agency is sorely needed. This proposed Hawaiian fauna specialty group should include field biologists from zoos, universities and museums, as well as others with proven expertise on Hawai'i's native and introduced fauna. What is currently missing in Hawai'i is dialogue among experts with differing perspectives. This will allow for accurate and realistic recommendations to be made. Legitimate consensus and cooperation can only benefit Hawai'i's precious living natural resources.

Brown Anole, *Anolis sagrei.* Male displaying.

THE BROWN TREE SNAKE CONTROL GROUP
by Paul Breese and Jean DeMercer-Breese

A great deal of local and national media attention has recently been given to the environmental and economic disaster on the island of Guam caused by the Brown Tree Snake *(Boiga irregularis)*. The Brown Tree Snake is a native of New Guinea and adjacent islands. It was unintentionally introduced to Guam following World War II, probably as a stowaway in military cargo. Once established, this mildly venomous, rear-fanged snake, which may grow to be over ten feet (3 m), created an environmental and economic disaster on Guam. These unusually aggressive nocturnal snakes have eliminated most of the native forest bird species on Guam. Additionally, these arboreal serpents cause over one hundred power outages on the island each year by crawling over electric wires and touching their bodies against both positive and negative terminals at the same time. The numbers of Brown Tree Snakes on Guam, which exceed fifty per acre in some locations, are the highest known population density of any land snake anywhere in the world.

In recent years, seven Brown Tree Snakes have been found on Oʻahu, six on or near airport runways and one more in a military cargo storage warehouse many miles from the airport. Four were alive. However, there is no known established population of these snakes in the state of Hawaiʻi at this time (1996).

The Brown Tree Snake Control Group (BTSCG) was founded in 1990 by former long-time Honolulu Zoo Director Paul Breese in order to help prevent this extremely damaging, highly unusual, adaptable species of snake from becoming established in Hawaiʻi. He invited several of his reptile specialist colleagues and William Thompson, the former Head of the State of Hawaiʻi Department of Land and Natural Resources, to join him to create the BTSCG. At that time, the inspection and control programs for the Brown Tree Snake both in Guam and on Hawaiʻi were in need of great improvement. The BTSCG has worked effectively in a non-confrontational manner to network with many governmental officials and private agencies in the development of workable programs and in securing funds for ongoing Brown Tree Snake control, inspection and research measures.

In 1991, supported by a grant from the Hawaiian Electric Company, three members of the BTSCG spent two weeks on Guam. They met with federal, territorial, and military officials involved with the Brown Tree Snake, including Guam Governor Joseph Ada. The three BTSCG members were: Sean McKeown, Curator of Reptiles at Chaffee Zoological Gardens in Fresno, California, who formerly held the same post at the Honolulu Zoo and is a recognized authority on island reptiles; Dr. Donald Hunsaker II, Biology Professor at San Diego State University, who has conducted extensive reptile research in Hawaiʻi and elsewhere; and Paul Breese, BTSCG founder. The primary objective of the group was to evaluate existing inspection procedures utilized when aircraft and container freight cargo leaves Guam and arrives in Hawaiʻi. These

Paul Breese holding an adult Brown Tree Snake captured on Guam.

experts made specific recommendations for improving the inspection procedures and for initiating more intensive techniques for detecting these snakes.

Breese made an additional trip to Guam with Tim Ohashi, Hawai'i Animal Damage Control Program Director of the U.S. Department of Agriculture, to assist in establishing much improved Brown Tree Snake control and inspection programs. A very effective additional detection method was the utilization of specially trained dogs to locate Brown Tree Snakes in cargo and aircraft. The use of these dogs began in Guam in 1993 after being strongly recommended by the BTSCG.

Scientists believe that the extremely high survival of Brown Tree Snakes on Guam is likely due to the absence of any effective predators there. The existing government programs for control and inspection are vital to help prevent Brown Tree Snakes from leaving Guam.

A major activity of the BTSCG is to provide Hawai'i's congressional delegation and state legislators with current, accurate evaluations of the various Brown Tree Snake control and research programs. Based on these evaluations, the BTSCG also makes recommendations of the need for further methods of control, research, and expansion of existing programs. Due primarily to the congressional support of Hawai'i Senators Daniel Inouye and Daniel Akaka, over one million dollars per year has been appropriated for Brown Tree Snake control since the BTSCG has become involved. Prior to 1990, there were no allocations of funds specifically designated for the detection and control of these snakes. This funding has been appropriated to help keep the Brown Tree Snakes from arriving in Hawai'i, other Pacific islands, and the U.S. mainland. It is likely that the Brown Tree Snake could also thrive in southern California and in several of the states bordering the Gulf of Mexico, and, in particular, Florida.

The BTSCG is an outstanding example of how reptile specialists can work cooperatively with various governmental agencies and legislators to help develop and promote programs to assist with important biological problems, in this case, the on-going task of preventing Brown Tree Snakes from invading and becoming established in Hawai'i and elsewhere.

In addition to continuing Brown Tree Snake inspection, detection, and control programs, the urgent need **now** is intensive research to explore and develop biological control methods to drastically reduce the Brown Tree Snake numbers on Guam.

———————————■———————————

DISTRIBUTION MAPS
Frogs and Toads

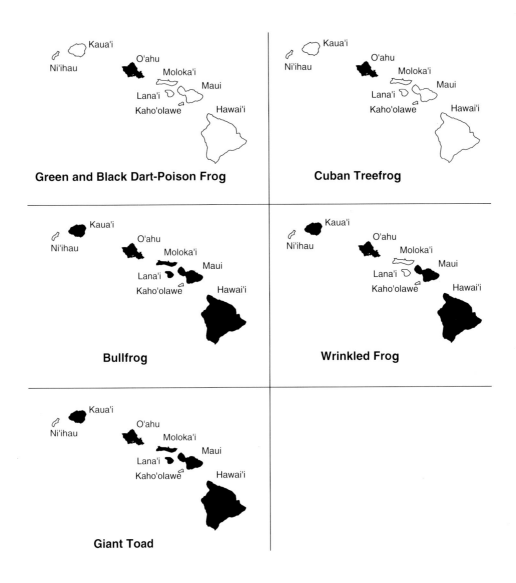

Green and Black Dart-Poison Frog

Cuban Treefrog

Bullfrog

Wrinkled Frog

Giant Toad

Lizards
Iguanid, Anoles, and Old World Chameleon

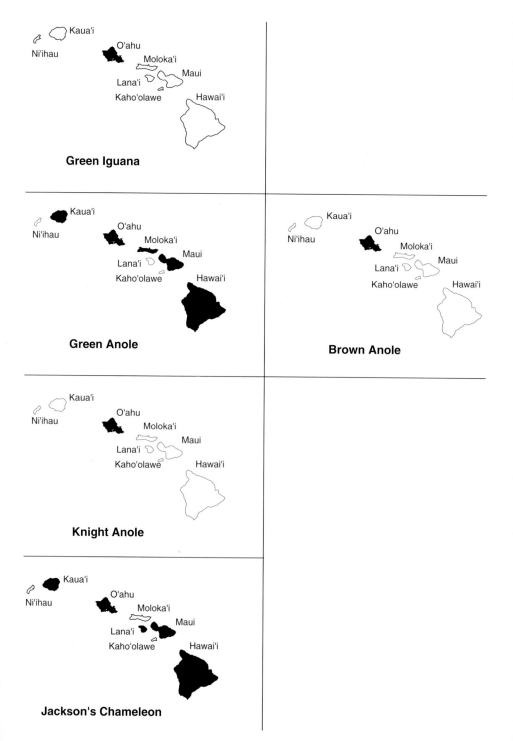

Geckos

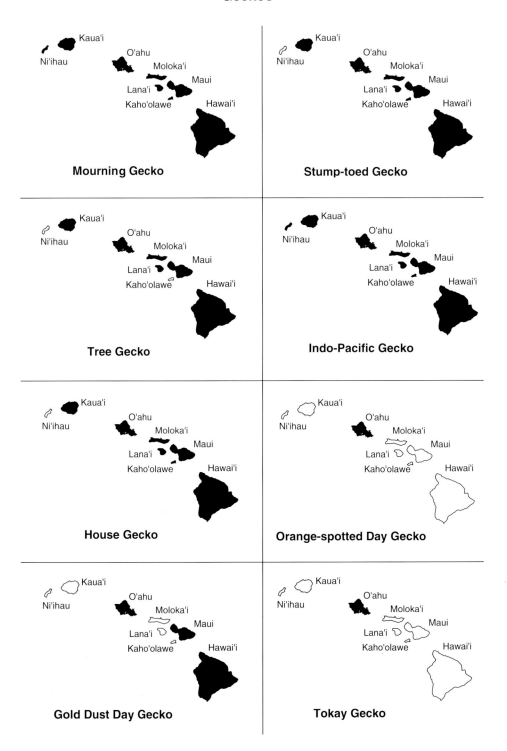

Mourning Gecko

Stump-toed Gecko

Tree Gecko

Indo-Pacific Gecko

House Gecko

Orange-spotted Day Gecko

Gold Dust Day Gecko

Tokay Gecko

Skinks

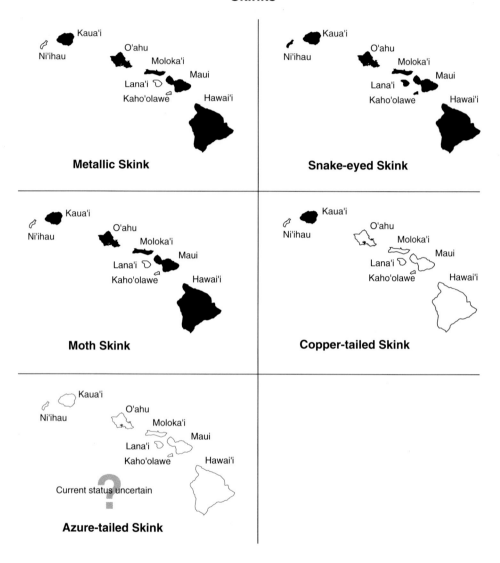

Metallic Skink

Snake-eyed Skink

Moth Skink

Copper-tailed Skink

Current status uncertain

Azure-tailed Skink

Snakes

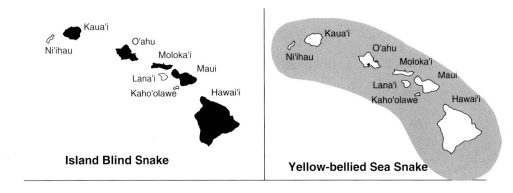

Island Blind Snake

Yellow-bellied Sea Snake

Turtles
Freshwater and Marine

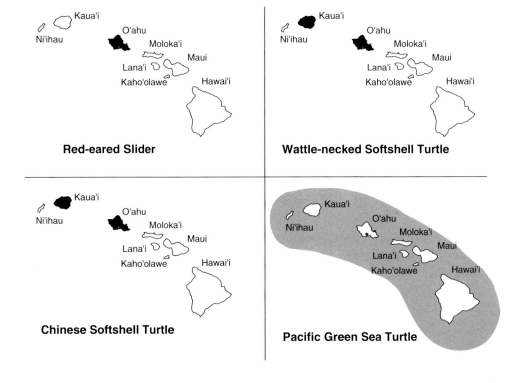

Red-eared Slider

Wattle-necked Softshell Turtle

Chinese Softshell Turtle

Pacific Green Sea Turtle

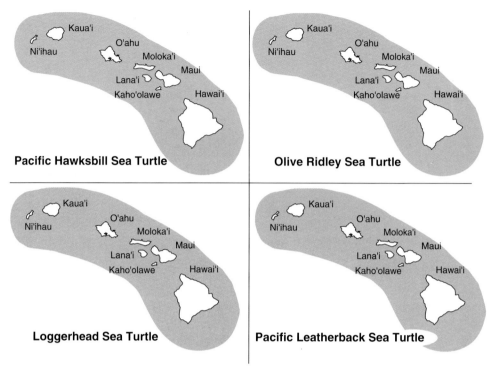

Pacific Hawksbill Sea Turtle

Olive Ridley Sea Turtle

Loggerhead Sea Turtle

Pacific Leatherback Sea Turtle

George Balazs, Hawaii's premier marine turtle conservation biologist, examines a nesting Pacific Green Sea Turtle, *Chelonia mydas agassizii,* at French Frigate Shoals in the Leeward Hawaiian Islands.

GLOSSARY

A

Acclimation. The adjustment by an animal to its surroundings when in captivity.

Amplexus. The sexual embrace of a female amphibian (frog or salamander) by a male amphibian.

Anterior. Toward the head or forward end of an animal.

Antibiotic. A general term for a drug that will kill or control pathogenic bacteria.

Anuran. From the Greek "tailless" and referring to all frogs and toads, which comprise the order Anura.

Arboreal. Dwelling in shrubs or trees.

B

Bask. To place the body or section of the body in a position directly exposed to the sun.

C

Calcareous. Consisting of or containing calcium carbonate.

Carapace. The upper shell of a turtle.

Chelonian. A turtle; any member of the order Testudines (Chelonia).

Cloaca. The common chamber in reptiles and amphibians into which the digestive, urinary, and reproductive canals discharge their contents, and which opens to the exterior through the anus or vent.

Clutch. The eggs laid by a single female amphibian or egg-laying reptile in one breeding effort.

Courtship. Ritualized behavioral interactions between males and females that precede and accompany mating.

Crepuscular. Active at twilight periods (dusk or dawn).

D

Desiccation. The process of drying out. In amphibians and reptiles, it may apply to both eggs and the actual animal if air moisture levels become too low.

Dewlap (throat fan). Loose skin hanging from the throat of some lizards, which is used for display. When extended, the throat fan is typically larger and/or more colorful in males.

Display. A specific pattern of behavior involved in communication between animals. It includes any of the senses such as vision, hearing, touch and smell.

Diurnal. Active during the daytime.

Dorsal. Of or pertaining to the back or upper surface of the body.

Dorsolateral. Of or pertaining to the upper sides of the body.

E

Ectoparasite. A parasite that inhabits the outer surface of an organism, e.g., a mite or tick.

Ectothermic. Regulating the body temperature by means of outside sources of heat, such as the sun (= the out-dated term "cold-blooded").

Endemic. Confined to a certain area, region, group of islands or continent and found nowhere else.

Endothermic. Regulating the body temperature by means of an internal regulating mechanism so as to produce a more-or-less constant body temperature (= warm-blooded).

Estivation (also aestivation). A prolonged inactivity during the hottest periods of the year.

Family. A taxonomic category ranking below order and above genus.

Femoral pores. Small openings, containing a waxlike material, on the underside of the thighs in some species of lizards.

F

Fossorial. Adapted for and leading primarily a burrowing existence.

G

Genus (pl. genera). A taxonomic category above species and below family. In a scientific name, the genus appears before the species name, and the first letter is always capitalized.

Gestation. The period of development or carrying of embryos by the female of a species within the body.

Granules. Tiny, flat scales.

Gravid. A female bearing eggs or young, ordinarily in the oviducts (= pregnant).

Gregarious. Tending to congregate into groups.

Gular fold. Fold of skin across the rear of the throat, well developed in certain lizards.

H

Hemipenis (pl. hemipenes). One of the grooved, paired copulatory organs (double penis) found in male lizards and snakes. The hemipenes are elongated, rounded pouches which are turned outward during copulation. Only one is used at each mating. When not in use, the hemipenes are sheathed in the lateral portions of the ventral area of the tail.

Herpetology. The study of reptiles and amphibians.

Herptile. Any individual reptile or amphibian.

I

Indigenous. Occurring or living naturally in a particular region or place, but not restricted in distribution to that area (=native).

Interspecific. Occurring between members of different species.

Intraspecific. Occurring between members of the same species.

Island supertramp. An animal that, upon becoming established in an island environment in which it is not native, does major irrevocable damage to the fauna or flora where it has been introduced.

J

Jacobson's organ. One of the primary sensory organs in snakes and many lizards. This organ is located in the roof of the mouth and is used to perceive odors and chemical substances.

Juvenile. A young, not sexually mature individual, sometimes displaying proportions and coloration which differ from that of the adult.

L

Labial. Of or pertaining to the upper or lower lip.

Lamina (pl. laminae). A horn-like plate overlying the bony layer of the shell of many turtles.

Larva (pl. larvae). The immature individual between egg and adult stages which differs in appearance from its parents and which typically must pass through metamorphosis before assuming the adult characteristics.

Lateral. Of or pertaining to the side.

M

Melanistic. Having an abundance of black pigment, resulting in an all-black or unusually dark animal; the opposite of albinism.

Metamorphosis. A marked change from larval to adult form or structure, and usually also in habits and food, as when a tadpole changes into a frog.

N

Neotenic. Retaining the larval form and appearance throughout life but capable of reproduction.

Nocturnal. Active primarily at night.

Nominate. Referring to the first or originally described form or type of a given species.

Nuptial pad. Rough, dark pigmented skin on the fingers of male amphibians which develop during the breeding period and aid the male in holding the female during amplexus.

O

Omnivorous. Feeding on both animal and plant material.

Oviparous. Reproducing by means of eggs that hatch outside the body of the female.

Ovoviviparous. Reproducing by means of eggs that have a shell, but which hatch inside the female before or just before laying so as to produce living young.

P

Pantropic. Occurring or distributed throughout the tropical regions of the world.

Parotoid. One of a pair of large external wartlike glands located on each side of the back of the head in toads and particularly well developed in toads of the genus *Bufo.*

Parthenogenesis. Reproduction by means of the development of an unfertilized egg. Involves the development of eggs from virgin females without fertilization by spermatozoa.

Parthenogenic. Produced by parthenogenesis (=unisexual).

Pathogenic. Disease causing. Examples include bacteria and many viruses.

Pectoral. Of or pertaining to the chest.

Pelagic. Of or living in the open sea.

Pharynx. The portion of the alimentary canal between the cavity of the mouth and the esophagus.

Plastron. The lower shell of a turtle.

Pleurodont. Having the teeth located on the inner edge of the jaw, as in iguanid lizards.

Postanal scales. Scales located on the ventral surface posterior to the anus. Typically in male iguanid lizards, two or more of these scales are enlarged.

Preanal scales. Scales located on the ventral surface anterior to the anus. In males of some geckos and certain other lizards, these scales may have enlarged pores that secrete a waxlike substance.

Predation. Obtaining food through consumption of prey animals which may be either vertebrates or invertebrates.

Prehensile. Adapted for grasping or seizing, especially by wrapping around, as in the tail of certain lizards and snakes.

R

Resource partitioning. Referring to the utilization of separate or different portions of the same habitat so as not to compete directly for existing resources. This term may be applied to separate species, to different age groups within a species, or, less commonly, to males and females of the same species.

Reticulations. A network-type pattern of markings.

Riparian. Living at the edge or in close proximity to a river, stream or similar fresh water body.

S

Scale. A thin, flattened platelike structure forming the major part of the surface covering of reptiles and certain other vertebrates.

Scute. Any enlarged scale of a reptile which may also be referred to as a 'plate' or 'shield.'

Sexual dichromatism. Sexually dimorphic in color. Typically in reptiles, the adult males are the most colorful.

Sexual dimorphism. A difference between males and females of the same species in color, form, or structure.

Shell length. The direct or straight-line length of a turtle's carapace, measured along the midline from front to rear.

Shield. A plate. In reference to turtles, any of the "plates" or "scutes" of horn that cover the shell in most species.

Snout-vent length (SVL). The direct or straight-line length of a reptile, amphibian or other animal as measured from the anterior tip of the snout to the posterior tip of the vent.

Species. A population of animals that naturally interbreeds to produce fertile offspring. Traditionally, the fundamental unit of classification.

Subadult. A young individual that is older and/or larger than a juvenile, but which has not yet achieved full adult size. Subadults may be capable of breeding although, if social, have not as yet obtained a high rank within the group.

Subcaudal. Beneath or on the ventral surface of the tail.

Subspecies. When a species is distributed over a geographic area with diverse environmental conditions, the members in one section of the range may differ slightly in form or color from those in another section. Each subdivision is known as a race or subspecies.

Substrate. The material which is used on the bottom of a terrarium, such as soil, newspaper or bark.

Sympatric. A term applied to two or more populations of animals that occupy the same or overlapping geographical areas.

T

Tadpole. The aquatic larva of a frog or toad which later, through the process of metamorphosis, develops into an adult.

Taxon (pl. taxa). A specific taxonomic group or entity such as a species, subspecies or genus.

Terrarium. A vivarium without standing water.

Terrestrial. Living primarily on land or on flat surfaces.

Territorial. Defending an area so as to exclude other members of the same or other species.

Threat display. A social behavior to indicate territorial ownership or aggressive intent. This behavior may be directed towards members of the same species or individuals of different species. It may take the form of specific color changes, tail-waving and/or head movements.

Total length (TL). The direct or straight length of a reptile, amphibian or other animal as measured from the anterior tip of the snout to the posterior tip of the tail.

Tympanum. The eardrum. In many frogs and toads, it is externally well-developed and is larger in males than in females.

V

Vent. The ventral opening of the cloaca which serves as the terminus of both waste discharge and the reproductive canal; in snakes and lizards the vent is considered the division between the body and tail.

Ventral. Of, or pertaining to the underside of the body.

Vertical pupil. A vertically elliptical pupil of the eye that is especially useful to animals active at night.

Vestigial. Referring to a small and degenerate or imperfectly developed bodily part or organ that remains from one or more fully developed in an earlier stage of the individual, in an ancestral form, or closely related forms.

Visual signals. Many amphibians and reptiles use these distinctive behaviors in establishing territory and in courtship. Visual signals are extremely important in intraspecies interactions and usually involve specific movements of the head, body and tail.

Vivarium. An enclosure for keeping or raising and observing animals indoors.

Vocalization. The act of uttering vocal sounds. Frogs vocalize, and male frogs have a range of calls. Geckos also have well-formed vocal chords and a diverse vocal repertoire. Geckos of both sexes are able to make a series of auditory sounds or vocalizations.

Vocal sac. An inflatable pouch on the throat of frogs and toads that swells with air and serves as a resonating chamber when these anurans call (croak) and collapses at the end of the call.

A SHORT LIST OF REFERENCES FOR FURTHER STUDY

Balazs, George, H. 1976. *Hawaii's Seabirds, Turtles and Seals.* Honolulu: World Wide Distributors, Ltd.

Balazs, George H. 1986. Ontogenetic Changes in the Plastron Pigmentation of Hatchling Hawaiian Green Turtles. Journal of Herpetology 20(2):280–282.

Berger, John and Sean McKeown. 1979. Hawaii's Green Iguana. Honolulu Magazine. May:113.

Brock Vernon. 1947. The Establishment of *Trionyx sinensis* in Hawaii. Copeia 2:142.

Brown, Susan G. and J. O'Brien. 1993. Pseudosexual and diminance behaviour: their relationship to fecundity in the unisexual gecko, *Lepidodactylus lugubris.* J. Zool., Lond. 231:61-69.

Brown, Susan G. and Patrick K. Duffy. 1992. The Effects of Egg-laying Site, Temperature, and Salt Water on Incubation Time and Hatching Success in the Gecko *Lepidodactylus lugubris.* J. of Herp. 26(4):510-513.

Brown, Susan G. and Toni Jean Y. Sakai. 1988. Social Experience and Egg development in the Parthenogenic Gecko, *Lepidodactylus lugubris.* Ethology 79:317-323.

Brown, Walter C. 1954. Notes on Several Lizards of the Genus *Emoia* with Descriptions of New Species from the Solomon Islands. Fieldiana. Chicago Nat. Hist. Museum 34(25):263–276.

Bryan, Jr., E. H. 1932. Frogs in Hawaii. The Mid-Pacific Magazine. XLIII(1):61–64.

Bryan, William A. 1915. *Natural History of Hawaii.* Honolulu: Gazette Company, Ltd.

Bull, J. J. and R. C. Vogt. 1979. Temperature-dependent Sex Determination in Turtles. Science 26:1186–1188.

Burghardt, Gordon M. and A. Stanley Rand, eds. 1982. *Iguanas of the World: Their Behavior, Ecology, and Conservation.* Park Ridge: Noyes Publication.

Burns, Barry and George V. Pickwell. 1972. Cephalic Glands in Sea Snakes *(Pelamis, Hydrophis* and *Laticauda).* Copeia 3:547–559.

Case, Ted J. and Douglas T. Bolger. 1991. The Role of Introduced Species in Shaping the Distribution and Abundance of Island Reptiles. Evolutionary Biology 5:272–290.

Cobb, J. N. 1902. Commercial fisheries of the Hawaiian Islands In *Report of the United States Commissioner of Fish and Fisheries for the Year Ending June 30, 1901.* Washington, D.C.: U.S. Government Printing Office. pp.381–499.

Cochran, Doris M. and Coleman J. Goin. 1970. *The New Field Book of Reptiles and Amphibians.* New York: G. P. Putnam's Sons.

Crews, David. 1979. The Hormonal Control of Behavior in a Lizard. Scientific American 241(2):180–187.

de Vosjoli, Philippe. 1993. *The Green Iguana Manual.* Lakeside: Advanced Vivarium Systems. 175 pp.

Duellman, W. E. 1993. *Amphibian Species of the World: Additions and Corrections.* University of Kansas Museum of Natural History's Special Publication 21:372 pp.

Ernst, Carl H. and Roger W Barbour. 1989. *Turtles of the World.* Washington, D. C. Smithsonian Institution Press. 313 pp.

Fischer, Harvey I. 1948. Herpetological Notes. Copeia 1:69.

Hunsaker, Donald II and Paul Breese. 1967. Herpetofauna of the Hawaiian Islands. Pacific Science 21(3):168–172.

Ineich, Ivan and George R. Zug. 1991. Nomenclatural Status of *Emoia cyanura* (Lacertilia, Scincidae) Populations in the Central Pacific. Copeia 4:1132-1136.

Iverson, John B. 1992. *A Reviewed Checklist with Distribution Maps of the Turtles of the World.* Richmond, Indiana. Privately printed. 363 pp.

Jennings, Mark R. 1987. Impact of the Curio Trade for San Diego Horned Lizards *(Phrynosoma coronatum blainvillii)* in the Los Angeles Basin, California: 1885–1930. Journal of Herpetology 21(4):356–358. SSAR.

Jennings, Mark R. and Marc P. Hayes. 1985. Pre-1900 Overharvest of California Red-legged Frogs *Rana aurora draytonii)*: The Inducement for Bullfrog *(Rana catesbeiana)* Introduction. Herpetologica 41(1):94–103.

Jordon, David S. and Barton W. Evermann. 1903. The aquatic resources of the Hawaiian Islands; part I—The shore fishes. Bull. of the U. S. Fish Commission. 23:527–528.

LaRivers, Ira. 1948. Some Hawaiian ecological notes. The Wasmann Collector 7(3):85–110.

Lazell, James D., Jr. 1989. Kaho'olawe: Hawaii's Largest Uninhabited Island. The Explorer's Journal. September.

Mayer, Greg and James D. Lazell, Jr. 1992. Identity and Distribution of the Introduced *Anolis* lizard of Hawaii and Other Pacific Islands. Bull. Ecol. Soc. of America 73(2):265.

McGregor, Richard C. 1904. Notes on Hawaiian Reptiles from the Island of Maui. Proceedings of the U.S. Natl. Museum, Vol. XXVIII:115–118. Washington, D.C.

McKeown, Sean. 1978. *Hawaiian Reptiles and Amphibians.* Honolulu: The Oriental Publishing Company. 80 pp.

McKeown, Sean. 1982. *Hawaiian Animal Life Coloring Book.* Honolulu. Oriental Publishing Company. 93 pp.

McKeown, Sean. 1991. Jackson's Chameleons in Hawaii are the Recently Described Mt. Kenya Subspecies, *Chamaeleo jacksonii xantholophus.* Bull. Chicago Herp. Soc. 26(3):49.

McKeown, Sean. 1993. *The General Care and Maintenance of Day Geckos.* Lakeside: Advanced Vivarium Systems. 143 pp.

McKeown, Sean, 1995. Jackson's Chameleons *(Chamaeleo jacksonii)*: Natural History, Captive Management and Breeding chapter In *Chameleon Keeper's Reference Series. Vol. I. Care and Breeding of Panther, Jackson's, Veiled, and Parson's Chameleons.* Philippe deVosjoli and Gary Ferguson, eds. Lakeside: Advanced Vivarium Systems.

McKeown, Sean and Robert G. Webb. 1982. Softshell Turtles in Hawaii. Journal of Herpetology 16(2)107–111.

Oliver, James A. and Charles E. Shaw. 1953. The Amphibians and Reptiles of the Hawaiian Islands. Zoologica 38:65–95.

Petren, Kenneth, Douglas T. Bolger and Ted J. Case. 1993. Mechanisms in the Competitive Success of an Invading Sexual Gecko over an Asexual Native. Science. 259:354–358.

Petren, Kenneth and Ted J. Case. 1994. Gecko Power Play in the Pacific. Natural History Magazine 9:53–60.

Pickwell, George V. 1971. Knotting and Coiling Behavior in the Pelagic Sea Snake *Pelamis platurus (L.)*. Copeia 2:348–350.

Pickwell, George V. 1972. The Venomous Sea Snakes. Fauna 4 (July/August):17–32. R. M. Ryan Publisher

Pritchard, Peter C. H. 1979. *Encyclopedia of Turtles.* Jersey City: T. F. H. Publications, Inc. 895 pp.

Shaw, Charles E. and Paul L. Breese. 1951. An Addition to the Herpetofauna of Hawaii. Herpetologica 7:68.

Snyder, John Otterbein. 1917. Notes on Hawaiian Lizards. Proceedings of the U.S. Natl. Museum 54:10–25. Washington, D.C.

Stejneger, Leonard. 1899. The Land Reptiles of the Hawaiian Islands. Proc. U. S. Natl. Museum 49:124–125.

Svihla, Arthur. 1936. *Rana rugosa* Schlegel. Notes on the life history of this interesting frog. Mid-Pacific Magazine 49(2)124–125, figs. 1–3.

Tayless, John. 1968. Serpents in Paradise. Pacific Discovery. XXI(3):24–26.

Tinker, Spencer Wilkie. 1938. *Animals of Hawaii, a Natural History of the Amphibians, Reptiles, and Mammals Living in the Hawaiian Islands.* Honolulu: Tongg Publishing Company. 188 pp.

Walsh, Matt. 1990. Gold Dust Day Gecko in Hawaii. Bull. Chicago Herp. Soc. 25(11):209.

Wilson, Larry D. and Louis Porras. 1983. The Ecological Impact of Man on the South Florida Herpetofauna. The University of Kansas Museum of Natural History and World Wildlife Fund — U.S.

Zug, George R. 1991. *The Lizards of Fiji: Natural History and Systematics.* Honolulu: Bishop Museum Press. 136 pp.

Metallic Skink, *Lampropholis delicata*.

INDEX

Chinese Softshell Turtle, *Pelodiscus sinensis.*

FROGS AND TOADS

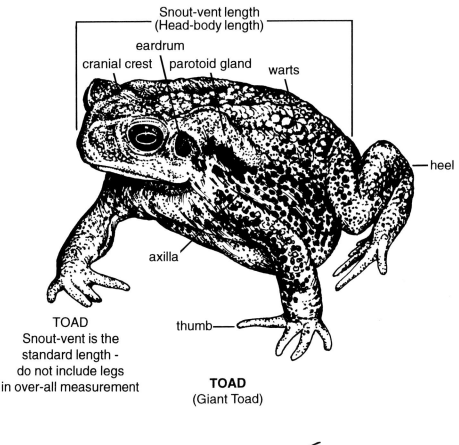

TOAD
Snout-vent is the
standard length -
do not include legs
in over-all measurement

TOAD
(Giant Toad)

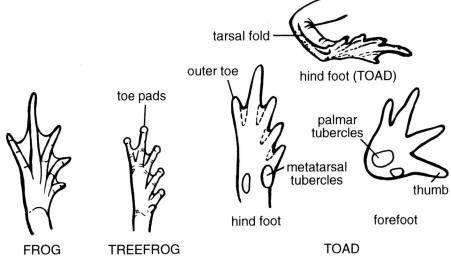

FROG   TREEFROG   TOAD

© *Drawings by Jane Bowden-Manente*

LIZARDS

S. McKeown

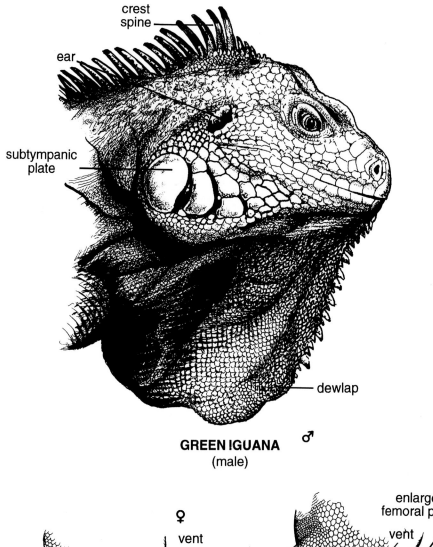

crest
spine

ear

subtympanic
plate

dewlap

GREEN IGUANA ♂
(male)

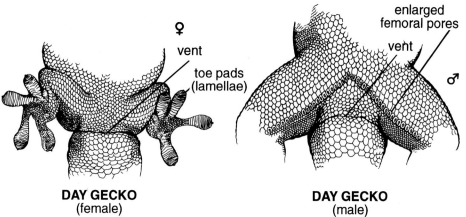

♀

vent

toe pads
(lamellae)

enlarged
femoral pores

vent

♂

DAY GECKO
(female)

DAY GECKO
(male)

© *Drawings by Jane Bowden-Manente*

TURTLES

GREEN SEA TURTLE

SCUTES
A = abdominal
AN = anal
C = costal
F = femoral
G = gular
H = humeral
I = inframarginal
M = marginal
N = nuchal
P = pectoral
V = vertebral

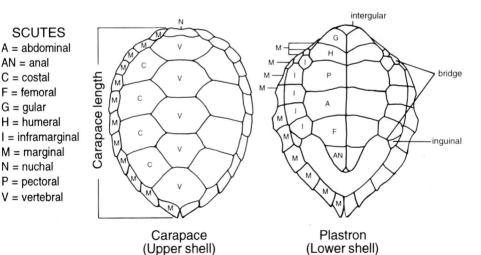

Carapace
(Upper shell)

Plastron
(Lower shell)

TURTLES
Carapace length is the standard length - do not include head,
legs or tail in over-all measurement

© *Drawings by Jane Bowden-Manente*

Yellow-bellied Sea Snake, *Pelamis platurus*.

VENOMOUS

About the Author

Widely recognized as the foremost authority on Hawaiian herpetology, Sean McKeown is internationally respected for his work with reptiles and amphibians from island ecosystems: their natural history, ecology, conservation, captive management, and breeding.

A frequently published author on herpetological topics, Sean is associate editor for the American Federation of Herpetoculturists (AFH), and a working member of the International Union for the Conservation of Nature (IUCN). He served for over 20 years as Curator of Reptiles at the Honolulu Zoo and Chaffee Zoological Gardens.

A Field Guide to Reptiles and Amphibians in the Hawaiian Islands represents over 20 years of field research by the author on the lizards, snakes, turtles and frogs occurring in the Aloha State.